Shrubs and Small Trees

THE ROYAL HORTICULTURAL SOCIETY

Shrubs and Small Trees

Simon Akeroyd

LONDON, NEW YORK, MUNICH,
MELBOURNE, DELHI

SENIOR EDITOR Zia Allaway
SENIOR DESIGNER Rachael Smith
DESIGNER Alison Shackleton
EDITOR Simon Maughan
MANAGING EDITOR Anna Kruger
MANAGING ART EDITOR Alison Donovan
PICTURE RESEARCH Lucy Claxton, Mel Watson
PRODUCTION EDITORS Clare McLean, Jonathan Ward

PHOTOGRAPHY Peter Anderson

First published in Great Britain in 2008 by
Dorling Kindersley Ltd
Penguin Books Ltd
80 Strand
London WC2R 0RL

2 4 6 8 10 9 7 5 3 1

A CIP catalogue record for this book is available
from the British Library.

ISBN 978 1 40532 790 9

Printed and bound by Star Standard, Singapore

Discover more at
www.dk.com

Contents

Using trees and shrubs

Forming the backbone of a garden, trees and shrubs are by far the most versatile of all plant groups. Most are long lived and provide colour, structure and texture throughout the whole year, creating permanent props to stage displays of flowers, foliage, berries and winter interest. Trees and shrubs are also essential to our ecology, providing a habitat for our diminishing wildlife. And whatever the size or style of your garden, from vast woodland to tiny courtyard, there's a range of shrubs and trees to suit. Leaf through this chapter for inspiration and exciting ways to use these wonderful plants.

Seasonal colour: winter stems, bark and flowers

Nature provides an abundance of colour in winter. Attractive berries and fruits linger on the branches while frosty catkins glint from trees. Deciduous plants denuded of their leaves now show off their colourful trunks and stems.

Pictures clockwise from left

A winter woodland Contrasting colours at different heights can be produced with trunks and bare stems during winter. The use of just three or four variations is usually enough. Here, the dark mahogany red of the ornamental cherry, *Prunus serrula*, is a stunning feature on its own, but it looks even better when combined with the stark contrast of the white birch, *Betula utilis* var. *jacquemontii*, and the bright yellow stems of the golden willow, *Salix alba* var. *vitellina*.

Garden ghosts and fiery embers The bright red winter stems of these dogwoods (*Cornus alba*) will create a striking impact in any garden, particularly when the light from the low winter sun catches them. Interplanted among ghostly white birches, the effect is even more dramatic. Evergreen shrubs with variegated foliage give subtle colour and texture.

Brilliant berries No winter planting would be complete without berrying plants. Some, like this *Skimmia japonica*, combine their bright fruit with contrasting evergreen foliage. Berries provide welcome interest during winter, as well as food for wildlife. Other plants worth considering include the white-berried snowberry (*Symphoricarpos*), the fiery orange-reds of pyracanthas and sea buckthorn (*Hippophae*), female hollies, and the large red rosehips of *Rosa rugosa*.

Winter flowers Winter isn't just about brightly coloured stems and berries. Lots of shrubs brave the elements and produce flowers, many of which have intoxicating scents. These large yellow flower spikes of *Mahonia japonica* have an exquisite winter perfume, and they really stand out against the dark and glossy evergreen leaves. Other plants that produce scented winter flowers include wintersweet (*Chimonanthus*), witch hazel (*Hamamelis*), *Daphne bholua*, *Viburnum* x *bodnantense*, and Christmas box (*Sarcococca*).

Seasonal colour: spring blossom, flowers and fruit trees

There's always a sense of anticipation in the air for gardeners as spring heralds the start of a new growing season. The garden awakes from dormancy, the leaves unfurl, and spring blossom colours the landscape.

Pictures clockwise from top left

Heathery heaven This heather, *Erica* x *veitchii* 'Exeter', starts its flowering season in the bleak cold of winter and continues right through to the middle of spring. Bees adore its dense clusters of sweetly scented white blooms as it's one of the first flowers of the season, and therefore a good source of early nectar.

Japanese cherry blossom Reminiscent of brightly coloured clouds, Japanese cherry trees are smothered in delicate flowers in spring. The Japanese love these trees so much that they hold celebrations called hanami, where people picnic and party under the blossom. Shown here, *Prunus incisa* 'Kojo-no-mai' is a lovely choice for a small garden with light red buds that open to reveal pale pink flowers. Flowering beneath is *Erica carnea* 'Springwood White', the winter heath. Most fruit trees have pretty spring blossom, including plums, apples, and quinces.

Rhododendron flower power Spring is the highlight for many woodland gardens with camellias, magnolias and rhododendrons all bursting into bloom. This effect can be replicated in much smaller spaces by adopting a simple planting combination of two or three spring-flowering shrubs, such as the bright rhododendrons seen here. Rhododendrons and camellias are evergreen shrubs that require acid soil and prefer dappled shade.

Spring jewels There are many shrubs that emerge in spring with an understated charm. *Stachyurus chinensis* is one such plant; a stunning, graceful shrub that is not seen in gardens as often as it deserves. The subtle but beautiful pale yellow flowers are particularly valuable because they appear very early in the season when little else is in flower; they hang from the plant like jewels on a necklace in late winter and early spring before the leaves emerge.

Seasonal colour: summer flowers and fruit

Long evenings and warm weather make summer the season for outdoor living. Since all the preparation work is now complete, you can sit back and enjoy the fruits of your labours as flowers unfold, fruit ripens, and leaves glisten.

Pictures clockwise from top left

Colourful courtyard Patios need to be at their best now as you will spend more of your time here in summer. Trees and shrubs offer height and a sense of enclosure, as well as bountiful flowers, like this pink hydrangea and white buddleja. Containers provide further planting opportunities for shrubs and herbaceous plants.

Modern roses Traditionally, roses were planted in single beds where the different varieties could be compared and admired. Modern designs use them in mixed borders, where they mingle with other flowers.

Mophead mixes The highlight of late summer with their large, showy flowers, hydrangeas are reliable flowering shrubs for mixed or shrub borders.

Summer bounty Decorate your garden with fruits, such as currants, gooseberries, strawberries, cherries, plums, pears, and early apples – all will fit into a small plot.

Climbing bouquets These beautiful classic roses can be trained up posts or into trees to add height and make an eye-catching feature. The choice is huge, so it is easy to match one to the existing planting scheme.

Autumn colour: berries, nuts, leaves, and fruit

Take advantage of autumn colour to ensure the growing season ends with a grand finale. Choose ornamentals for their showy leaves and berries, and fruit trees for their spectacular harvest.

Pictures clockwise from centre

Autumn explosion Gardens can be a firework of colour as the leaves of autumn take centre stage. These colours stand out even better when they are deliberately planted to contrast with one another. In this picture, maple, vine, and mahonia leaves all play their part, along with the subtle russet tones of the sedum flowerheads, which will stay on the plant well into winter.

Bunches of berries Gardens are not just for people, they are for wildlife too, and birds adore the red berries of *Viburnum opulus*. This is a wonderful plant for an informal hedge; the leaves also turn a beautiful red in autumn.

Exquisite colour Not all leaves are a riot of bright colour in autumn. Other trees take on more refined, subtle hues, like this yellow birch (*Betula alleghaniensis*) with its beautiful buttery yellow foliage, or the common beech (*Fagus sylvatica*), which turns a glorious coppery colour.

Wild about nuts With the onset of the autumn harvest, ripening crops, like these hazelnuts, hang on to the last vestiges of summer sunlight. Squirrels and other animals will try to raid the trees before winter arrives.

Gardens for year-round interest

By using evergreen structures, focal points, and strong design elements a garden can look good all year round.

Plants should be big, bold, and definitely beautiful if they are going to become permanent features of the landscape.

Pictures clockwise from left

Bare stems and box hedges Evergreen trees and shrubs, such as box, privet and yew, give a permanent framework through which seasonal interest can be interwoven. The focal point in this picture is *Viburnum rhytidophyllum*, a dense bush that is usually grown for its glossy foliage and long-lasting flowers and berries. Here, its canopy has been raised by removing the lower leaves and branches, which adds height and opens up the vista beyond. It also enables plants to be grown underneath, like this wavy-edged box hedge.

Strong shapes and colours Unusual features are great for placing a stamp of individuality in a garden. Architectural plants, such as this cloud-pruned conifer, will remain striking all year round. Consider other big and bold plants like palms, ornamental grasses, tree ferns, bamboos, yuccas, or large cordylines. Strong flower colours nearby, or painted walls or fences, can be used to underline the effect.

Focus on foliage Variegated forms of evergreen plants increase a gardener's colour palette and can include cream, white, silver, yellow and gold. This design has used *Euonymus fortunei* 'Emerald Gaiety' and the holly *Ilex aquifolium* 'Silver Milkboy'. A plain, green-leaved ivy in the foreground is being used as ground cover, while mind-your-own-business (*Soleirolia soleirolii*) is used instead of a lawn to produce an all-year-round carpet of green. The whole planting is enhanced by the careful placing of flowering shrubs between the evergreens, and the bright stepping stones that disappear beyond the shrubbery; these create intrigue by drawing the eye towards the back of the garden.

Woodland gardens

A leafy glade provides a place to unwind and take shelter from the midday sun. Some trees and shrubs create shade, while others thrive in it, providing the potential for a wonderful mix of plants.

Pictures clockwise from top left

Woodland sentinel Ferns are archetypal woodland plants, most growing close to the ground, but this tree fern (*Dicksonia antarctica*) forms a fibrous trunk with its mass of roots, lifting it well above the forest floor. With strong architectural qualities, it makes a superb focal point for a small woodland garden.

The path least travelled Woodland paths should look enticing, natural, and follow the contours of the garden. If there is room, create a circular path, even if it simply goes around a mature tree or a piece of rustic furniture. For the surface, use natural products like bark or wood chippings.

Spring flowers The peak season for a woodland garden is spring, when flowering bulbs carpet the forest floor just before the deciduous trees open their leafy canopies. Woodland shrubs, like this yellow azalea, should not be overlooked as they also come out in force during spring. Other spring performers include camellias and magnolias.

Make the most of foliage A woodland garden needs canopies at different heights, to create tiers of interest. Variegated shrubs, such as this dogwood, are useful in a small space as the foliage is bright and eye-catching, and it casts dappled shade under which woodland bulbs like anemones, cyclamen, trilliums, and bluebells will grow.

Formal and topiary gardens

The orderly arrangement of formal gardens is defined by straight lines and symmetrical planting. There are many ways to introduce these elements, but one of the most pleasing is to use tightly clipped shrubs and evergreen topiary.

Pictures clockwise from top right

Grand avenue Rows of trees, such as these variegated poplars, accentuate the direction of interest and lead the eye. The arch in the hedge frames the sundial giving us a tantalising glimpse of another part of the garden. Smaller gardens can use avenues of shorter plants like standard bays or photinias.

Formal yet contemporary Gardens can be formal while at the same time look contemporary and chic. The very modern architectural planting of this garden frames the simple rectangular water feature which forms the garden's focal point, decking at the front, and the small formal lawn.

Variation on a theme While most formal designs are on flat, level ground, this one demonstrates how a classic style of gardening can be turned on its head with a little ingenuity. The Tudors would have created intricate knot gardens with these low evergreen hedges, but here they are presented like a miniature patchwork of undulating fields. The beds are filled with block colours of low-growing ground-cover plants, such as camomile, thyme, feverfew, and cotton lavender.

A topiary set piece The concept of formality can be taken to extremes if straight lines and tightly clipped plants are allowed to dominate, which is further emphasized here by blue sleepers. Dwarf conifers are chosen because they are low maintenance and serve many uses, from low hedging and ground cover to simple structures and intricate topiary work.

Relaxed symmetry Formal rules can be applied in a more relaxed manner. Just a few clipped box shrubs and two lollipop holly trees are used in this small courtyard to make it symmetrical, while the rest is given over to a more relaxed, informal mix of tulips, bedding plants, and the architectural shrub, *Fatsia japonica*.

Wildlife gardens

As natural habitats are increasingly lost to development, the more important gardens are becoming to wildlife. Trees and shrubs have a vital role to play in the wildlife garden, as they provide food and shelter for a rich diversity of creatures.

Pictures clockwise from far left

Bees, birds, and butterflies Many flowering shrubs like this buddleja are magnets for bees and butterflies. Caterpillars feed on the foliage of nearby plants and should be tolerated so long as they don't do too much damage, as they are a valuable source of food for birds and mammals. Bees do an essential job of pollinating flowers, from which fruit, nuts, and berries arise. Red mason bees are easily catered for by drilling long narrow holes into pieces of old wood and hanging them from a branch or a wall.

Rotten opportunity Many types of wildlife are attracted by rotting tree stumps or piles of logs in a garden. Stack thick prunings or logs in a quiet, damp corner under the shade of a tree or shrub, and soon a whole host of wildlife will begin moving in.

Berries for birds There are plenty of berrying trees and shrubs to choose from, but it is best to pick species or varieties of native plants, as this is what the local wildlife are used to. Holly trees with their prickly leaves also provide cover from predators.

Water for wildlife A pool or pond will attract a host of wildlife, including breeding insects, which in turn encourage birds, bats, hedgehogs, and amphibians. Birds and small mammals will also use the water for drinking and bathing. The pond doesn't have to be big – a large puddle will attract wildlife – but ensure it has sloping sides to allow creatures to get in and out easily.

Trees in the garden Woodlands are rich habitats for wildlife, and most small gardens can accommodate at least one small tree, underplanted with shrubs, perennials, and bulbs. Try to disturb the area as little as possible so that birds, mammals and insects can move in and make their homes there.

Contemporary gardens

Modern living often requires low maintenance gardens. Trees and shrubs usually require far less annual work than other plants, while at the same time offering year-round interest.

Pictures clockwise from top left

Leaves and stripes Flowers aren't always required to create colour as this mixed border demonstrates. The bright leaf blades of the grasses contrast beautifully with the rounded, dark green leaves of the shrub and the textured foliage of the Japanese maple, which is just beginning to reveal its autumn colour. Japanese maples are ideal trees for restricted spaces in contemporary gardens owing to their small size and tolerance of dappled shade. Maple foliage comes in a wide range of hues from green through to yellow, orange, and purple.

Sculpted structure Although the trees and shrubs in this garden are not the first things that catch the eye, they form an integral part of its design. Of these, the central components are the clipped box spheres and multi-stemmed maple to one side of the studio. A white-flowered loquat tree planted on the opposite side and silver birches in the background are a more subtle touch. Not only do these trees and shrubs complement the herbaceous planting beautifully, but they also bring all the elements together, including the studio.

The hidden garden This garden is subdivided into "secret" compartments hidden within box hedges, behind fences, and under a canopy of formal, umbrella-pruned plane trees. It makes an ideal place to retire on a hot day and shows how trees and shrubs can be used as screens to partition a garden.

Modern poolside planting This garden illustrates the importance of height in a garden, a requirement that is easily met by the planting of trees or shrubs. Height lifts the eye, and adds an extra dimension to a landscape. This wooden shelter achieves that aim, but it would be totally out of balance with the rest of the garden if it was not for the magnolia and cercis shrubs planted on either side.

Courtyards and roof terraces

Trees and shrubs are impressive plants and make an impact even in the smallest of spaces. For people living in the city, planting opportunities may be restricted and confined, which can lead to unusual and innovative solutions.

Pictures clockwise from top left

Hornbeam quartet These four clipped hornbeam trees take up almost no space at ground level in this small garden, and show how large trees can be incorporated into a garden without using up much of the living space. Fastigiate trees, which have a naturally narrow shape, are also useful for small and confined spaces. This patio feels larger than it is because of the small formal pool that reflects the movement of the sky and the hornbeams as they gently sway in the wind.

Creative containers Trees and shrubs that are grown in containers and frequently clipped will be restricted in their size, allowing more plants to be grown in a small area. Plants also grow more slowly in pots, so there is less pruning and maintenance, although woody plants in containers can be clipped into topiary or bonsai, if you have the time to create and care for them. One of the advantages of growing plants in pots is that they can be moved around to vary the display from time to time, and you can take them with you when you move house.

Cool greens Very often the best designs are the simplest, using shrubs to create subtle variations of a single colour while also adding interesting shapes and textures into the mix. The box tree standards and the golden stems of the bamboo create height at the back of this seated border, and are softened by the wonderful textural qualities of the variegated pittosporum shrubs. *Fatsia japonica* in the bottom left has superb architectural qualities with its large, evergreen leaves.

Leafy living room If a small garden has room for just one tree, then *Acer griseum* is a worthy contender for that place. It has superb cinnamon-coloured, flaking bark and wonderful autumn colours. Here, it is used in a container within a small bed of leafy heucheras and ferns.

Themed gardens

A garden with a theme allows you to indulge in a subject you feel passionate about, as well as giving it your individual stamp. The woody plants you choose will be one of your first major decisions.

Pictures clockwise from top left

Ramshackle old vineyard Grape vines and roses make a good marriage in this garden, and follow a long tradition of growing rose bushes at the ends of rows of vines. When choosing varieties of grape and rose pick those that will produce strong and healthy growth – look for plants with an RHS Award of Garden Merit (AGM) as a guide. You can also include trees with an exotic look, such as hardy palms, cordylines, and cypresses.

Zen garden Trees and shrubs have an important role to play in Zen philosophy, but the emphasis is not on plants and structures, it's about imparting a sense of stillness and contemplation. Rocks, gravel, and sand are symbolic elements that represent mountains and oceans.

Cottage effects The relaxed branching habit of many shrubs and trees, such as this robinia, lend themselves perfectly to the informality of cottage gardens.

Exotic themes Outdoor living would need to be a prominent theme for such a garden, with trees and shrubs chosen to create the look and feel of a warm country. Many Mediterranean plants would suit, as well as those with bold foliage like palms, catalpas, and hardy bananas.

Getting started

To get the best from your trees and shrubs it's essential to know how to grow and nurture them. In this chapter learn how to test and improve the soil in your garden, and discover what plants are most likely to thrive there. Also follow the advice on choosing healthy plants when out shopping, and planting and staking them when you get home. Finally, if you're feeling creative, you can make a willow fence, a simple parterre, or an elegant plaited standard bay tree using the step-by-step instructions.

What is a tree?

Trees are perennial plants that usually form a single upright woody trunk. They are generally larger than shrubs and can be evergreen or deciduous, coming in a range of sizes from tiny maples to giant redwoods.

Conical trees

The trunks of conical-shaped trees, typical of many conifers and a few broadleaved plants, usually extend right up to the top of the tree and have horizontal branches growing from them almost down to ground level. Their overall form is cone-shaped. Fastigiate or columnar trees are even narrower and are great for adding height into small gardens.

Planting suggestions
- *Carpinus betulus* 'Fastigiata'
- *Chamaecyparis lawsoniana* 'Columnaris'
- *Cupressus sempervirens*
- *Juniperus communis* 'Compressa'
- *Taxus baccata* 'Fastigiata'

Maintenance tips Very little care required, but be aware that some conifers get large very quickly.

Weeping trees

Trees with branches hanging downwards are referred to as weeping. These make attractive, graceful trees and there are many choices for a small garden. They are ideal as a feature in their own right but can also be used in borders to create shade for woodland flowers.

Planting suggestions
- *Betula pendula* 'Youngii'
- *Fagus sylvatica* 'Purpurea Pendula'
- *Morus alba* 'Pendula'
- *Prunus pendula* 'Pendula Rubra'
- *Pyrus salicifolia* 'Pendula'
- *Salix purpurea* 'Pendula'

Maintenance tips Remove any upright growth as it appears, and trim back branches that trail on the floor. The crown can get congested and should occasionally be thinned.

Standard trees

This is the most common shape, and describes a tree that forms a single trunk that divides further up, with branches stretching out vertically or horizontally. It is mainly broadleaved trees that have this habit, but some conifers, such as yews and pines, also grow like standards. Shapes vary greatly, from upright to spreading.

Planting suggestions
- *Acer pensylvanicum*
- *Betula utilis* var. *jacquemontii*
- *Pyrus calleryana*
- *Malus domestica* 'James Grieve'
- *Malus floribunda*
- *Sorbus aucuparia*

Maintenance tips Due to the top-heavy nature of young trees, they will need to be staked on planting (*see pp.38–41*). Some trees naturally shed their lower branches as they grow, while others have their lower branches removed (known as "crown lifting") to reveal more of the trunk. In some cases, the lower branches are left so that the tree's natural shape can be enjoyed.

Many conifers form a cone shape naturally. All they need is room to grow.

Weeping willows bear catkins in spring and can be underplanted with shade plants.

With an upright habit, the silver birch is a classic standard tree for gardens.

What is a shrub?

Shrubs produce multiple stems from ground level and rarely have a central trunk. Except for very tender shrubs, which may die back over winter, they have a permanent, woody structure throughout the year.

Multi-stemmed shrubs

Shrubs are a popular choice for a small garden as they form the backbone of any design with their permanent framework and structure. Their multi-stemmed habit also makes them useful as screens and hedges. Many are grown for their attractive foliage or flowers, but some can be used purely for their mass of colourful winter stems.

Planting suggestions
- *Buddleja globosa*
- *Hydrangea macrophylla*
- *Leycesteria formosa*
- *Potentilla fruticosa*

Maintenance tips Trim back early flowering shrubs once the display is over, and late shrubs in early spring. Cut down winter stems close to ground level in early spring.

Wall shrubs

Some shrubs benefit from the support of a wall or fence, either due to their slightly lax habit or because they need extra shelter and warmth. Many can be trained in this manner simply to enhance a wall or to make the most of a small space.

Planting suggestions
- *Abutilon megapotamicum*
- *Acca sellowiana*
- *Ceanothus arboreus*
- *Chaenomeles x superba*
- *Euonymus fortunei*
- *Garrya elliptica*
- *Kerria japonica* 'Pleniflora'

Maintenance tips Most wall shrubs need to be trained onto a support and pruned regularly to keep them to size. Slightly tender plants benefit from a fleece on very cold nights.

Ground-cover shrubs

Some shrubs naturally sprawl along the ground, often referred to as a prostrate habit. They are used to cover bare patches of ground and prevent weeds from germinating. Some produce attractive berries, while others can be grown for their flowers or foliage, and there are types for both sun or shade.

Planting suggestions
- *Arctostaphylos uva-ursi*
- *Euonymus fortunei*
- *Gaultheria procumbens*
- *Hedera helix* 'Glacier'
- *Hypericum calycinum*
- *Juniperus squamata* 'Blue Carpet'
- *Leptospermum rupestre*
- *Rosa* Swany

Maintenance tips For quick results, plant ground-cover shrubs in groups of three to five, or even more if it is a large area that is to be covered. Some can be invasive and will need regular cutting or chopping back, so choose carefully and seek advice before you plant. Make sure that all weeds are eliminated prior to planting.

Dogwoods and willows make striking multi-stemmed shrubs for winter display.

Wall shrubs like this ceanothus do a very good job of hiding drab walls.

This prostrate juniper shows clearly the spreading nature of a ground-cover plant.

Checking site and soil type

Right plant, right place is an important maxim when choosing trees and shrubs, so check what type of soil you have and how much sun your garden receives. You can then draw up a list of plants that will thrive in your garden.

Clay and loamy soils can be rolled into a sausage shape. If the clay content is high, you will be able to join up the ends to form a ring.

Clay soil This is probably the hardest type of soil to manage. Clay soils do not drain well in winter, yet in summer they bake dry and crack. To discover if you have a clay soil, roll a sample between your hands. If it can be moulded into a ring, then it is clay soil.

Sandy soil Due to their sandy content, these soils drain easily, so water and essential soluble plant minerals and nutrients are not retained. To test for sandy soil, roll the soil around in your hands. If it feels gritty or dusty and cannot be rolled into a ball then it is sandy soil.

Silty soil Like sandy soils, these also drain easily. When handled, they have a silky texture and cannot be rolled.

Loam It is very unusual to have a soil made up of just one of the elements above; most are a mixture. Loam is the happy medium – it is dark brown in colour and holds moisture for a while before it slowly drains away. It can be rolled into a sausage but breaks when bent into a ring.

Sandy soil falls apart if you try to roll it into a ball, and it has a distinctive gritty or dusty texture.

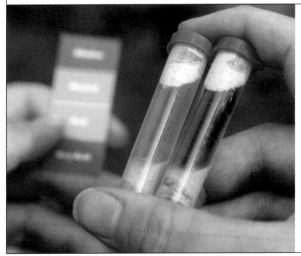

The acid test As well as knowing the composition of your soil, it is just as important to know its acidity. The most reliable method of checking is to use a soil pH testing kit. They are easy to use and can be bought from any good garden centre. You will be instructed to select soil samples from different areas of your garden, and as you do this remember to take samples from at least 2cm (¾in) below the soil surface, as this is where the roots grow. Most kits will then ask you to mix the soil with distilled water and a pH indicator, which turns the solution a particular colour; check the colour against the chart in the pack to find out your pH reading. A reading of 7 is neutral; anything above is alkaline, and anything below is acidic. The optimum is between 5.5 and 7.5.

Check your aspect Sunlight is just as important to plants as having the correct soil to grow in. All plants need sunlight to photosynthesize, but some require much less than others. Rhododendrons and skimmias, for example, are naturally woodland plants, and they are therefore best suited to quite shady conditions. Rosemary and lavender bushes, however, prefer sites that are hot and dry, so a sunny site is the place for them.

When scrutinizing the aspect of a garden, don't forget that shade and sun fall in different places during the day, so an area that is a sun trap first thing in the morning may well be quite cool and shady by late afternoon. Also consider shade cast by large trees, fences, and walls, and remember that the sun is higher in the sky in summer than it is in the winter. It often pays to live with a new garden for a year in order to observe these subtle changes, before you undertake any major and expensive planting of trees and shrubs.

Make the most of microclimates The speed at which the soil warms up and the temperature is maintained during the year depends on soil type and aspect. This can create different microclimates in the garden. Sandy soils warm up more quickly than clay, as do sites that receive a lot of sun. In the northern hemisphere, such a site would be facing south or south-west. A south-facing slope is even hotter as the plants are angled towards the sun. South-facing walls absorb heat during the day and radiate this back at night, protecting slightly tender plants from cold and frosty nights. Conversely, the coolest, shadiest part of the garden would be a north-facing wall, which will receive no direct sunlight at any time of the year.

This garden is planted to take advantage of its aspect. Sun-lovers are used in the centre of the garden, where they get the most light.

The walled end of the garden gets the late-afternoon sun, and acts as a sun trap. Here, slightly tender trees and shrubs can be grown.

Improving soil In terms of pH, it is extremely hard to alter the soil. On a small scale the ground can be made more alkaline by adding lime, or more acidic by adding ericaceous compost, sulphur chips, or pine needles. This is expensive in a large area, so it's best to work with what you've got and grow plants that are suited to the pH. The same could be said of sandy soils. Although any soil can be dramatically improved by digging in lots of organic matter to help it retain nutrients and moisture, this can be washed away very quickly on sand, so it is easier to choose plants that will thrive in dry conditions, such as herbs or prairie plants. Improve clay soils by digging in plenty of horticultural grit or sharp sand and organic matter like well-rotted manure or compost.

Choosing shrubs and trees

There is a vast choice of woody plants in garden centres and nurseries, so it pays to understand what you are buying and how to choose a healthy plant, as quality can vary. Restrict yourself to plants that suit your garden's conditions.

Container-grown trees and shrubs

Most garden plants are supplied this way. They can be planted at any time of year, and you can see the plant in growth rather than relying on information on the label. On planting, the roots have a tendency to grow in a circle, which can eventually strangle the plant, causing it to die.
Buying tips Always read the label to check that you have enough space for the fully-grown plant, and that it suits your soil and intended position. Check that the plant is container-grown and not recently dug up and potted on.
Planting tips Tease out the roots to prevent them from circling, and soak the root ball thoroughly before planting.

Bare-root trees and shrubs

Only a few types of plant, such as fruit trees, hedging plants and roses, are available in this form. You will find them for sale, often via mail order, from late autumn to late winter when the plants are dormant. They are freshly dug from the nursery fields and taken to the plant centre where they are temporarily planted into a large bed of compost. Bare-root plants are usually much cheaper than their container-grown equivalents and also more likely to establish well, as their roots are not all curled up in a pot.
Buying tips Only deciduous trees or shrubs tend to be available bare-root, and they must only be bought when the plants are dormant. Make sure the roots are well developed and even; plants with lopsided roots are likely to fail. Prepare your intended site before purchasing bare-root plants because they will need to be planted as soon as possible.
Planting tips If you can't plant immediately, then heel in the plant by digging a hole and covering the roots and base of the stem with soil. Plant the tree or shrub at the depth that it was at when growing in the nursery field. There should still be the original soil mark right at the base of the trunk. Try to plant them in their final positions as soon as possible, before the arrival of spring.

Health checks before you buy

Trees and shrubs can be expensive to buy, so make sure you buy the healthiest plant possible from a reputable supplier. Specialist nurseries are great for rare and unusual plants. Busy retail outlets can be good as they usually have a fast turnover of stock, which means that their plants are not left languishing for months in a tiny pot.

General check Avoid lopsided plants and those with damaged branches. Look for lush, healthy, balanced and well-proportioned growth.

Roots Reject plants with congested roots or with hardly any roots at all. Dead, fibrous roots can indicate neglected or drought-stressed plants.

Diseases and pests Be wary of blemished or discoloured foliage and check for pests. Holes and notches in leaves may indicate vine weevils.

Choosing containers for shrubs and trees

Almost any tree or shrub can be grown in a container. A huge range is available, and often the trick is to match the container with the shape, colour, and texture of the plant, as well as the style of your garden or house. First and foremost, however, make sure that any container is fully frost resistant and has adequate drainage holes.

Man-made terazzo Elegant and contemporary, this mix of marble chippings and granite is durable, yet smooth and cool to the touch.

Clay This traditional material may be glazed or natural. It's not always frost-proof, and as clay absorbs moisture, more watering is often needed.

Stone Heavy but hard wearing, there are many styles from modern to antique. Eventually stone pots can become covered in moss and lichen.

Planting a tree

A well-planted tree will reward you with years of healthy growth. Don't plant the tree too deeply, because it may cause the trunk to rot, and stake it to prevent wind-rock.

1 Before planting, clear the area of weeds and give the tree a good watering. Dig over any compacted soil. Container-grown trees can be planted at any time of year, but avoid periods of drought and frost.

2 Dig out a circular hole, approximately twice the width of the pot and to the depth of the root ball. Avoid digging over the bottom of the hole as the tree will sink after planting. Instead, puncture the base with a fork.

3 Scratch the sides of the hole with a spade or puncture them with a fork. This encourages roots to grow beyond the sides of the hole as they search for water and nutrients. The result will be a stronger tree.

4 Place the tree in the hole, then lay a stick or bamboo cane across the top to ensure that the upper surface of the root ball is level with or slightly above the ground. It may be easier to do this by removing the container first.

Planting a tree *continued*

5 Remove the container and scrape away any excess soil or compost from the base of the trunk, clearing it right back to the top of the root ball. Check over the roots, ensuring that there is no sign of vine weevil larvae (*see p.121*).

6 Pull the roots out that have grown around the edge of the root ball. This is to prevent them from growing in a circle, eventually strangling the plant. For particularly root-bound trees, some roots may need cutting with secateurs.

7 Place the tree in the hole and spread the roots out as evenly as possible. Start to backfill the hole, while an assistant holds the tree upright. Ask the assistant to gently shake the tree to ensure the soil fills any gaps.

8 Firm the soil as you backfill the hole. Firstly, use your fingers to push the soil between the roots, then once all the soil has been returned to the hole, use your foot, with toes pointing towards the trunk, to gently firm the tree in.

9 Drive in a wooden stake at an angle of 45 degrees leaning into the direction of the prevailing wind. Ask your assistant to hold the tree away from the stake while this is done to prevent any damage. (*See pp.44–45*)

10 Attach the tree to the stake using a tree tie and a spacer. These should be placed about one-third of the way up the tree. The spacer will protect the trunk from the stake, and the tie can be adjusted as the tree grows.

11 Water the tree in well. It will need regular watering during its first year, particularly during the summer. Consider placing a guard around the trunk if rabbits, deer, or other animals are likely to be a problem.

12 Mulch around the base of the tree. Use either wood chippings, landscape fabric, or both to suppress weeds and to retain moisture. To prevent rotting, make sure that any chippings are kept away from the base of the trunk.

Planting a shrub

Since shrubs are a permanent presence in the garden, they must be carefully sited and planted. You will then be able to enjoy their shape, structure and form throughout the year.

1 Measure out the distance from neighbouring plants to ensure that the shrub has enough space to grow. Prior to planting, thoroughly water the plant in its container, and dig over compacted ground.

2 Dig out a hole, about twice the width of the container and the same depth as the root ball, using the plant as a guide. Enrich the removed soil by mixing with well-rotted organic matter and controlled-release fertilizer.

3 Gently remove the shrub from the pot, pulling out roots from around the edge of the root ball. Place it in the hole, then gradually backfill, holding the foliage away from the ground so that it's not buried.

4 Firm in the plant using your fingertips. Prune back any dead or damaged branches to healthy wood and remove any that make the shrub look untidy. Water in well and mulch with well-rotted garden compost or bark chippings.

Staking trees and shrubs

A stake is used to support a tree during its early years. There are many ways to stake a tree, and just as many theories as to which are the best methods. Here are a few of the most commonly seen.

The best type of stake is made of sweet chestnut, but any treated softwood will suffice. Use a tree tie to attach the stake to the tree, and cushion it with padding to prevent rubbing. After a couple of years you can expect the stake to have done its job; by then the tree's root system should be strong enough to support itself.

Diagonal stake Avoid damaging the roots by staking at 45 degrees before or after planting. This is stronger than an upright stake but can be a trip hazard.

Upright stake Aesthetically pleasing, as it follows the direction of the tree trunk. Fine for bare-root trees if driven in prior to planting, but unsuitable for pot-grown trees as you will be unable to get the stake near the trunk.

Square stake It is much easier to tie a tree tightly to a round stake, but if a square stake is used, you can secure the tree tie with a strong nail to prevent the tie from slipping. Take care not to damage the bark with the nail.

Sturdy stake Large, mature trees need very strong supports on planting. This structure avoids damage to the rootball and is suitable for public spaces, but standard tree ties are not designed to fix trees to this type of stake.

Two-stake method Often used for top-heavy standard trees like bay, which can be prone to snap just below the head if placed in exposed, windy sites. The stakes have been painted black to make them appear less obtrusive.

Staking lax shrubs

Guy ropes Established trees that have been moved to a new site benefit from a system of wires attached high up the trunk. It offers good support but requires a large space and the wires can be a trip hazard.

Staking shrubs Climbing and rambling shrubs like roses benefit from modified stakes, such as posts, pillars, and tripods. They can be used to create height and beautiful focal points in a small space.

How to plant a fruit bush

No kitchen garden is complete without a fruit bush or two. Plant blackcurrants (*shown below*) deeply to encourage lots of healthy shoots. Other fruit bushes need planting with the top of the root ball at or just under the level of the soil.

1 Dig out a hole three times the diameter of the root ball. Use the plant as a guide. The ideal time to plant is in autumn when the soil is still warm, but container-grown plants can be planted at any time of year.

2 Mix into the removed soil lots of well-rotted organic matter and controlled-release fertilizer, at the recommended rate. Remove the plant from its pot and pull the roots out from around the edges of the root ball.

3 Place the plant in the hole and backfill. Use your fingertips to firm the soil around the plant. Most fruit bushes should be planted shallowly, but blackcurrants need to have the top of the root ball 3cm (1¼in) below soil level.

4 Cut all the shoots back to one bud above ground level after planting. This encourages new vigorous shoots. Water in well, and mulch around the plant with plenty of well-rotted manure.

Planting a line of fruit cordons

Cordons are single-trunked trees on dwarfing rootstocks, and they are ideal for packing lots of tasty varieties into small spaces, or along a fence or wall. Mix fruit varieties together to ensure good pollination and bumper crops.

1 Measure out 70cm (28in) between where each tree will be planted and mark with a bamboo cane angled at 45 degrees. Attach three horizontal wires, 60cm (24in) apart, to the fence or wall and fasten the bamboo canes to them.

2 Plant the trees at an angle of 45 degrees. Some roots may stick out as a result. Cut these back with secateurs so that they will be covered by soil when planted. Ensure the graft union (a scar or kink on the trunk) is above the soil.

3 Attach the trees to the canes using chain-link plant ties. Water the soil under the trees well and cover with a mulch of well-rotted manure, leaving a gap around each trunk. Cut the main stem back by one-third if it is spindly.

4 Remove the first year's blossom from the trees after planting to encourage strong root systems. Prune new growth back to two buds each year at the end of summer; this will keep the trees compact and productive.

Planting a rose

Roses are essential shrubs for the garden and have many uses. Prior to planting hybrid tea and floribunda bush roses, prune them back to five buds from the base of each stem.

Tip for success

The bud union is where the rootstock has been grafted to the top growth. Bury it below ground level. On heavy soils, however, plant it about 2.5cm (1in) above to prevent it from rotting.

1 Dig a hole about twice the diameter of the pot and about a spade's depth. Choose a site that is sunny, well drained, and has not been used for roses previously as this can lead to the replant disease known as rose sickness.

2 Mix the soil from the excavated hole with equal amounts of well-rotted manure or compost. Add a sprinkling of a mycorrhizal fungi inoculant, which encourages a healthy root system. Follow the instructions on the packet.

3 Place the rose in the hole and spread out the roots. Make sure that the bud union is about 4cm (1½in) below the level of the soil, using a horizontal cane to judge the depth. Backfill the hole, firming the plant in as you go.

4 Water in well and mulch around the plant with well-rotted manure. Apply a rose fertilizer in spring as the buds break from their dormancy; any earlier and the fertilizer will be washed away before it can be taken up by the rose.

Planting a tree in a container

If you are short of space, try growing a tree in a container. An apple tree, shown here, is a good choice as you can enjoy the blossom in spring and the fruit later in the year.

Tip for success

Apple trees should be grown on moderately dwarfing rootstocks such as M26 to restrict their size. Select a self-fertile variety or grow another variety nearby to ensure pollination.

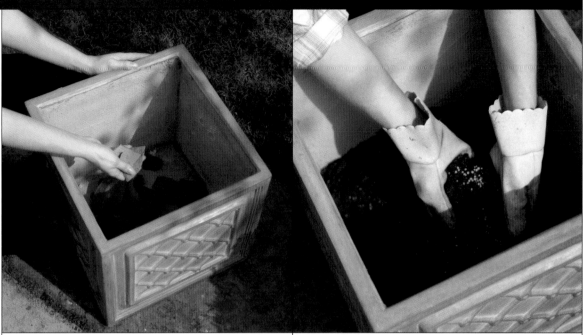

1 Buy a large container with drainage holes in the bottom. Place broken crocks, stones or polystyrene chunks in the bottom to prevent soil clogging up the holes. Soak the tree's roots in a bucket of water before planting.

2 Add a layer of loam- or soil-based potting compost to the bottom of the container and mix in controlled-release fertilizer at the manufacturer's recommended rate. Always use gloves when handling fertilizers and composts.

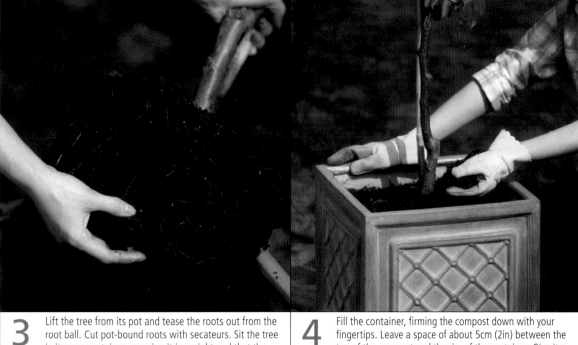

3 Lift the tree from its pot and tease the roots out from the root ball. Cut pot-bound roots with secateurs. Sit the tree in its new container, ensuring it is upright and that the root ball will be at its original planting level.

4 Fill the container, firming the compost down with your fingertips. Leave a space of about 5cm (2in) between the top of the compost and the rim of the container. Give it a good soak, and water well every day during the summer.

Planting a mixed deciduous hedge

An informal mixed hedge of deciduous flowering and fruiting shrubs makes a colourful, wildlife-friendly screen. Use bare-root plants as they are cheaper to buy.

1 Dig over the ground and clear any weeds from the site a few weeks prior to planting to allow the soil to settle. The best time to plant is in autumn as soon as bare-root hedging plants become available from nurseries.

2 Heel in the bare-root plants by digging a hole and covering the roots with soil. This will protect them prior to planting. Break up large clumps in the soil with a rake or fork, and remove any new weeds that have sprung up.

3 Reduce the fluffiness of the newly-raked soil by shuffling over the planting site with your feet. Lightly rake the soil over once again.

4 Mark the planting line with string, pegged down at each end. Double-rowed hedges need two lines about 40–60cm (16–24in) apart; they will provide more depth and shelter but are only suitable for larger gardens.

Planting a mixed deciduous hedge *continued*

5 Dig along the planting line, measuring out a space of 80cm (32in) between each plant. Either place a cane to mark where each shrub is going to be planted, or just measure and plant as you go.

6 Mix up the different bare-root plants so that they are planted in a random arrangement. Keep the roots of the plants covered when you are not using them; if the roots dry out the plants are much more likely to fail.

7 Begin to plant at the marked distances. Look for the original soil mark on the trunk of each plant as a guide to their planting depth; avoid planting any deeper. Roses are the exception, as deeper planting provides stability.

8 A quick method of planting bare-root trees is to place a spade into the soil, push it forward, and then slide the plant into the gap. Remove the spade, allow the soil to fall back around the plant, then firm in using your fingertips.

9 On a double-rowed hedge, plant the back row first then work on the front row. The idea is to create a staggered or zig-zag effect. Start 40cm (16in) in from the edge of the front row and then plant every 80cm (32in).

10 Check that the soil around all the plants is firmed in, and then water each plant thoroughly. Prune back the tips of any excessively tall or leggy shrubs to encourage new, bushy growth from the base of the plant.

Creating a parterre

Parterres are ornamental flower, herb or vegetable beds edged by low, tightly clipped evergreen hedges. This herb parterre is ideal outside a kitchen window.

Tip for success

Pinch out the growing tips of the edging plants to produce a compact, bushy hedge. Once established, they can be trimmed three times during the summer to keep them tidy.

1   Clear the site of weeds and then dig in plenty of horticultural grit to improve the drainage of the soil. Many herbs originate from Mediterranean-type climates and therefore thrive in such well-drained, dry conditions.

2   Rake the soil level and remove any large stones or roots of previous plants that might still be in the soil. The best tool for doing this job is a large-headed, stainless steel landscape rake.

3   Tread over the freshly cultivated soil in both directions to firm it and remove any air pockets. Keep your feet close together and firmly press your heels down into the ground. Gently rake over the soil again afterwards.

4   Place landscape fabric over the area to be planted. Dig the edges of the material into the soil to help hold it in place. The fabric will reduce the amount of watering and weeding needed later in the year.

Creating a parterre *continued*

5 Measure and mark out the pattern of the hedging with chalk to draw on the landscape fabric and pegs. Keep the pattern simple when designing for a small space, since too much intricacy will look messy and is hard to maintain.

6 With a sharp knife, cut slits into the landscape fabric approximately 20cm (8in) apart where the hedging plants are to go. Using a trowel or just your fingers, make planting holes in the soil and firm in the hedging plants.

7 Work around the pattern until all the hedging is planted. The shrubs in this pattern are box (*Buxus sempervirens*), but other suitable plants include *Lonicera nitida, Santolina chamaecyparissus* and lavender.

8   Arrange the herbs in their pots until you are happy with the design. Larger plants, like this bay tree in a terracotta pot, can be used to create a focal point. Cut the fabric and plant each herb carefully, as in step 6.

9   Brush away any soil that has fallen onto the fabric, then check over the plants. Remove any dead growth, or shoots or branches that have been damaged during planting. Water all the plants in well.

10   Place slate chippings over the surface of the fabric. This gives the parterre an attractive finish and hides the cuts that were made for planting. Other mulching materials can be used instead of slate, such as gravel or shingle.

Planting and plaiting a bay tree

Add a touch of formality to your garden by creating your very own standard plaited bay tree. It will look superb as a focal point in a herb garden or use a pair on either side of a doorway.

Tip for success

Multi-stemmed bay trees are sold at a fraction of the price of standard bays. Choose one with lots of tall, straight stems, and you may be able to make two standards from one shrub.

1 Cut through the root ball of a multi-stemmed bay with a spade to separate out the stems. If it's really root-bound use a pruning saw. Select three straight stems. Make sure that each stem has plenty of healthy roots attached to it.

2 Plant the three stems next to each other in the centre of a pot, and firm a soil-based compost around the roots. Remove the leaves from the lower two-thirds of the stems, leaving them bare with a head of foliage on top.

3 Plait the bare sections of the three stems tightly together, taking care not to snap them. When you reach the top, tie the stems firmly together with string or twine to hold them in place.

4 Trim off any uneven growth from the top to make a compact head, then water the tree in well. As the plant grows, keep the stems bare and pinch off the tips of the canopy with your fingers to create a bushy, rounded top.

Creating a living willow edge

Young willow stems are very pliable, allowing them to be manipulated into all sorts of living shapes and forms, such as this path edge. Stems can be cut yourself or bought via mail order.

Tip for success

Prune willow structures regularly or they will grow into trees. When buying stems, ask for a willow suited to the purpose.

1 Cut each stem close to a bud at the base to encourage better rooting after planting. Early spring is the best time to make a willow structure as the soil is starting to warm up and the stems are still bare and pliable.

2 Push the base of each stem about 20cm (8in) deep into prepared soil that is free of weeds. A dibber or bamboo cane can be used to make the hole first, if necessary. Willows prefer a moisture-retentive soil.

3 Bend each stem over to form a hoop and weave around itself so it keeps its shape. Tie with garden twine if the weave does not hold. Water the stems in well. By late spring the plants should be growing leaves.

4 Repeat this pattern along a path to form an attractive low hedge or edge, planting stems about 30–60cm (1–2ft) apart, depending on the size of the hoops. New growth can either be clipped or woven back into the structure.

Planting recipes

With so many beautiful trees and shrubs to choose from, drawing up a planting plan can prove difficult. To help you, here are some tried and tested planting recipes, showing the effects you can create using a range of seasonal and evergreen trees and shrubs. The symbols below are used in the recipes to indicate the conditions the plants prefer.

Key to plant symbols

   ♈   Plants given the RHS Award of Garden Merit

Soil preference

   ♦   Well-drained soil

   ♦   Moist soil

   ◊   Wet soil

Preference for sun or shade

   ☀   Full sun

   ☀   Partial or dappled shade

   ☼   Full shade

Hardiness ratings

   ✳✳✳   Fully hardy plants

   ✳✳   Plants that survive outside in mild regions or sheltered sites

   ✳   Plants that need protection from frost

Fruit border

Beautiful and edible, this mix of plants against a sunny wall combines a row of pear tree cordons (*Pyrus*) with colourful flowers and a low evergreen box hedge (*Buxus*). Flowering beneath the trees, perovskias are a good alternative to lavender with their generous sprays of purple flowers held high on white stems, and anthemis carpets the soil with its large white, nodding daisy flowers with golden centres. The silver, finely cut foliage of anthemis has a fruity scent and turns green in winter. The pear trees give spring blossom and late summer fruit.

Pyrus communis
❀❀❀ ◊ ◗ ☼

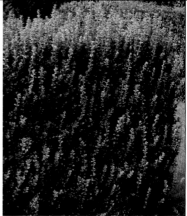

Buxus sempervirens
❀❀❀ ◊ ◗ ☼ ☼ ♆

Border basics

Size 1.5 x 5m (5 x 15ft)
Suits Narrow borders along boundaries
Soil Neutral, well-drained
Site Full sun

Shopping list

- 20 x *Buxus sempervirens*
- 3 x *Perovskia* 'Blue Spire'
- 9 x *Anthemis punctata* subsp. *cupaniana*
- 6 x *Pyrus communis* or *Malus domestica* (as cordons)

Planting and aftercare

Dig over the ground, remove all weeds, and rake it level. Allow the soil to settle for a few weeks, then start by planting the pear tree cordons at the back. To plant cordons, see page 47. Choose a selection of varieties that flower at the same time for heavy yields of fruit. Plant the box shrubs about 10cm (4in) back from the path and 30cm (12in) apart, and slot the flowering plants into the narrow space between the fruit cordons and the box hedge. Cut back the anthemis after flowering, and the stems of the perovskias in early spring to within three or four buds of the older wood. Fruit cordons need pruning in late summer by cutting the new growth back to two buds. Trim box in early summer.

Perovskia 'Blue Spire'
❦❦❦ ◊ ⛄ ♆

Anthemis punctata subsp. *cupaniana*
❀❀ ◊ ☼ ♆

Alternative plant idea

Malus domestica
❀❀❀ ◊ ◗ ☼

Mixed border in dappled shade

The dominant feature in this mixed border is the ornamental alder tree (*Alnus*) with its stunning, deeply cut leaves. Beneath the tree, in the light dappled shade created by its foliage, is a combination of two very different evergreen shrubs, and a spreading clump of herbaceous salvia. The box shrub (*Buxus*) is tightly clipped into a ball so that it acts as a foil to the sprawling greyish woolly foliage of the false dittany (*Ballota*). The salvia bears violet-blue flower spires through late summer.

Border basics

Size 5 x 5m (15 x 15ft)
Suits Large mixed border
Soil Well-drained
Site Full sun or dappled shade

Shopping list

- 1 x *Alnus glutinosa* 'Laciniata'
- 1 x *Buxus sempervirens* (as a ball)
- 5 x *Salvia nemorosa* 'Ostfriesland'
- 3 x *Ballota pseudodictamnus*

Planting and aftercare

Plant the alder tree towards the back of the border; if you have time to wait, buy a young tree as it will establish better. If you can't find 'Laciniata', try 'Imperialis' as it is similar but with more deeply cut leaves. Plant the ball of box about 40cm (16in) in from the edge of the border with the three ballotas around it: one on either side of the box and one behind it, leaving spaces of 30cm (12in). For the box ball, a cheaper option would be to buy a small shrub and shape it yourself. The salvias only tolerate some shade, so place them at the edge of the tree canopy where they will get more sun. The box will need clipping once a year in early summer, but the ballota can be allowed to sprawl, pruning back every couple of years to prevent it from getting leggy. Remove the salvia flower spikes as they fade to prolong the display.

Alnus glutinosa 'Laciniata'
✽✽✽ ◊ ◊ ☼

Buxus sempervirens
✽✽✽ ◊ ◊ ☼ ☼ ♈

Salvia nemorosa 'Ostfriesland'
✿ ✿ ✿ ◊ ◊ ☼ ☼ ♈

Ballota pseudodictamnus
✽✽✽ ◊ ◊ ☼ ☼ ♈

Modern rose garden

A stunning but simple planting scheme that uses the beautiful double red roses of 'Ruby Wedding' as its central feature. The other plants frame and highlight the rose, while also covering any bare, thorny stems at the base of the plant. The tiny bright leaves of the shrubby honeysuckle (*Lonicera*) make a stunning background for the deep red flowers, and the gold is reflected below by the euonymus. The dark blue and purple flowers of the catmint (*Nepeta*) and hebe increase the depth of vision, and the hydrangea extends the flower display into late summer.

Border basics

Size 3 x 2m (10 x 6ft)
Suits Mixed border
Soil Neutral, well drained
Site Sunny

Shopping list

- 1 x *Rosa* 'Ruby Wedding'
- 1 x *Hydrangea macrophylla*
- 3 x *Lonicera nitida* 'Baggesen's Gold'
- 5 x *Nepeta sibirica*
- 1 x *Euonymus fortunei* 'Emerald 'n' Gold'
- 1 x *Hebe* 'Midsummer Beauty'

Planting and aftercare

Add plenty of well-rotted organic matter to the soil before planting. The rose goes in the centre of the bed, planted deeply so the bud union is below soil level (*see pp.48–49*). The shrubby honeysuckles should be planted about 40cm (16in) behind the rose and the same distance apart, and the euonymus and hebe at the front of the border. The catmints can be placed randomly among the other shrubs, and the hydrangea belongs at the back. Remove dead flowerheads from the rose as they appear, but leave them on the hydrangea over winter. Trim the other plants back once a year – after flowering in the case of the catmint and hebe – to keep them tidy and compact.

Hydrangea macrophylla

Lonicera nitida 'Baggesen's Gold'

Nepeta sibirica

Rosa 'Ruby Wedding'

Euonymus fortunei 'Emerald 'n' Gold'

Hebe 'Midsummer Beauty'

Mediterranean mix

Mediterranean planting schemes not only give you a fantastic looking garden, but also offer a solution to climate change and hosepipe bans. A warm, sunny spot in the garden can easily be transformed by drought-tolerant shrubs, such as the lavender (*Lavandula*), rosemary (*Rosmarinus*), and cotton lavender (*Santolina*) used here. The focal point is the central olive tree (*Olea*) with its old, gnarled trunk and silvery leaves. A tree this size is expensive to buy, but much smaller trees can be purchased if you are willing to wait for them to grow. Myrtle or bay would make good, hardier alternatives. All the plants are evergreen and look great all year round.

Border basics

Size 3 x 3m (10 x 10ft)
Suits Gravel bed, rockery, herb garden
Soil Dry, well-drained, light
Site Full sun

Shopping list

- 5 x *Lavandula angustifolia*
- 5 x *Rosmarinus officinalis*
- 3 x *Santolina chamaecyparissus* or *Helichrysum italicum*
- 1 x *Olea europaea*

Planting and aftercare

Thoroughly weed the site and then dig in lots of horticultural grit to improve drainage. Plant the olive tree as a central feature, then randomly site the other shrubs around it to give a natural feel. No organic matter should be added as these plants prefer low-fertility soil. Finally, cover the bare earth with gravel, pebbles, and boulders to complete the effect. The plants will need watering in on planting but afterwards can be left to look after themselves. Cut back the lavender, rosemary and cotton lavender each spring to keep the plants compact, but avoid pruning back into old wood that has no buds growing from it.

Santolina chamaecyparissus
❄❄ ◊ ☼ ⚑

Olea europaea
❄❄ ◊ ☼

Rosmarinus officinalis
❄❄ ◊ ☼

Lavandula angustifolia
❄❄❄ ◊ ☼

Alternative plant idea

Helichrysum italicum
❄❄ ◊ ☼ ⚑

Shady poolside

This elegant, serene setting is created simply by grouping luxuriant foliage plants around the edge of a raised pool. Tree ferns (*Dicksonia*) are expensive but have a wonderful architectural structure that cannot be matched by any other plant. They provide height and drama while towering over the smaller golden male ferns (*Dryopteris*). Small maple trees (*Acer*) make attractive centrepieces, and the deeply dissected, purple leaves of this variety bring an interesting textural quality to the scene. The shady area beside the raised pool is a relaxing place to sit and watch the reflections of the leaves ripple across the surface of the water. Astilbe flowers come in white, red or pink, although they could be substituted with any shade-loving perennial plant.

Border basics

Size 5 x 5m (15 x 15ft)
Suits Courtyard, patio, or woodland
Soil Well-drained, moist
Site Dappled shade

Shopping list

- 3 x *Dicksonia antarctica*
- 1 x *Acer palmatum* var. *dissectum* Dissectum Atropurpureum Group
- 3 x *Astilbe* Cologne
- 3 x *Dryopteris affinis*

Planting and aftercare

Tree ferns should be planted at the same depth as they were in their pots. Soil preparation is not too important as their main root system is actually the fibrous network that forms the trunk. This should be sprayed over with water every few days during the summer. The maple likes well-drained and preferably slightly acidic soil, so add generous handfuls of ericaceous compost when planting. The astilbes thrive in dappled shade and moist soil. Plant the golden male ferns between the maple and tree ferns.

Dicksonia antarctica
❋❋ ◊ ◐ ☼ ☀ ♕

Acer palmatum var. *d.* Dissectum
Atropurpureum Group ❋❋❋ ◊ ☼

Astilbe Cologne
❋❋❋ ◊ ◐ ☼ ☼ ♕

Dryopteris affinis
❋❋❋ ◊ ☼ ♕

Conifer combo

Conifers can create a rich patchwork of textures, even in small spaces. As can be seen here, there is quite a variety of colour within this group of plants, including golds, blues, greys, yellows, and greens. Ornamental rocks and boulders add structure and a contrast in colour and texture. One of the benefits of a conifer garden is that the plants offer year-round interest for little maintenance; once planted they tend to look after themselves. When purchasing a conifer, always read the plant label carefully, because even though some are referred to as "dwarf", they may get quite large over time. If you have a small garden, you could grow them for five to ten years, almost like a short-term crop, before replanting with younger trees.

Border basics

Size 4 x 4m (12 x 12ft)
Suits Rock, conifer, or alpine garden
Soil Well-drained
Site Full sun or light shade

Shopping list

- 1 x *Picea pungens* Glauca Group
- 1 x *Picea abies* 'Ohlendorffii'
- 1 x *Platycladus orientalis* 'Aurea Nana'
- 1 x *Juniperus chinensis* 'Variegata'
- 1 x *Abies pinsapo*
- 1 x *Juniperus* 'Grey Owl'

Planting and aftercare

Plant the spruce (*Picea*) and fir trees (*Abies*) towards the back as they will eventually form large trees. The more compact plants should be placed where they won't get swamped by the larger trees. Position the juniper towards the centre as its spreading shape should fill the gap nicely. Mulch the beds with wood chip or bark. Very little aftercare is required; most conifers are best left unpruned, and trees that get too large for their space should be replaced.

Picea pungens Glauca Group
❄❄❄ ◐ ☼

Picea abies 'Ohlendorffii'
❄❄❄ ◐ ☼

Platycladus orientalis 'Aurea Nana'
❄❄❄ ◊◐ ☼ ♆

Juniperus chinensis 'Variegata'
❄❄❄ ◊◐ ☼ ☼

Abies pinsapo
❄❄❄ ◐ ☼

Juniperus 'Grey Owl'
❄❄❄ ◊◐ ☼ ☼ ♆

Spring collection

The central plant of this spring-time display is a deciduous Japanese snowball tree (*Viburnum*), named for its large and impressive white flower clusters. Behind stands the tall, leafy canes of the black bamboo (*Phyllostachys*) and the pretty purple flowers of the abutilon, which contrast well with the golden foliage of the mock orange (*Philadelphus*). This plant also has white flowers, and they are strongly scented. Below the shrubs is an underplanting of forget-me-nots (*Myosotis*) and other spring flowers.

Border basics

Size 4 x 3m (12 x 10ft)
Suits Mixed border, low maintenance
Soil Well-drained
Site Sunny, light shade

Shopping list

- 1 x *Abutilon* x *suntense* 'Ralph Gould'
- 1 x *Philadelphus coronarius* 'Aureus'
- 1 x *Viburnum plicatum* 'Mariesii'
- 1 x *Phyllostachys nigra*
- 5 x *Myosotis sylvatica*

Planting and aftercare

Site the mock orange and bamboo towards the back of the border about 2m (6ft) apart. The viburnum should be planted 1.5m (5ft) in front of these shrubs and underplanted with the spring flowers, which will self-seed and perpetuate year after year. Although some bamboos are spreading and invasive, the black bamboo is a good choice for a small garden, as it grows relatively slowly and remains fairly compact. This is a low-maintenance planting scheme that needs just the occasional prune to keep the size of the plants in check. The herbaceous underplanting will need to be tidied up after it has flowered and set seed. Pull up the dead material and add it to the compost heap.

Abutilon x *suntense* 'Ralph Gould'
❋❋ ◊ ◊ ☼

Philadelphus coronarius 'Aureus'
❋❋❋ ◊ ◊ ☼ ☼ ♆

Viburnum plicatum 'Mariesii'
❋❋❋ ◊ ◊ ☼ ☼ ♆

Phyllostachys nigra
❋❋❋ ◊ ◊ ☼ ☼ ♆

Myosotis sylvatica
❋❋❋ ◊ ◊ ☼ ☼

Summer shrub border

This border mixes shrubs of different foliage textures to extend the interest beyond the flower displays. The planting is commanded by the tall clerodendrum at the back of the scheme. It is probably the most striking of all the plants with its attractive greenish-white buds that open to white flowers and develop into decorative blue berries in autumn. The arching indigofera, with its tiny leaflets and pea-like pink flowers, is also a useful shrub in this position. The pink flowers are repeated on the spiraea towards the front of the border, while the potentilla produces bright orange flowers from late spring to late summer. The euphorbia is a classic architectural shrub, with unusual foliage and clusters of acid yellow, purple-centred flowers in early summer.

Border basics

Size 4 x 4m (12 x 12ft)
Suits Mixed or shrub border
Soil Well-drained, moist
Site Full sun, light shade

Shopping list

- 1 x *Clerodendrum trichotomum* var. *fargesii*
- 1 x *Spiraea japonica* Magic Carpet
- 1 x *Indigofera heterantha*
- 1 x *Euphorbia characias* subsp. *characias*
- 1 x *Potentilla fruticosa* 'Sunset'

Planting and aftercare

The clerodendrum is a large plant so give it plenty of space; it will also produce lots of ground shoots, which will require cutting back annually to ground level to prevent them from smothering the other plants. Near the front, plant the spiraea, euphorbia, and potentilla about 2m (6ft) apart. Summer-flowering spiraeas benefit from being cut right down in spring. The euphorbia can be cut back after flowering to keep it in shape and to remove dead stems, but avoid contact with the sap as it is a skin irritant.

Clerodendrum trichotomum var. *fargesii*
❀❀❀ ◊ ☼ ♛

Spiraea japonica Magic Carpet
❀❀❀ ◊ ☼ ♛

digofera heterantha
❋❋❋ ○ ☼ ♈

Euphorbia characias subsp. *characias*
❋❋❋ ○ ☼

Potentilla fructicosa 'Sunset'
❋❋❋ ○ ☼

Fiery autumn mix

Vibrant displays of fruit and foliage prove that autumn can be just as colourful as spring. To maximise the display, combine trees and shrubs that reveal different tints. In the garden opposite, the yellowing leaves of silver birch (*Betula*) form the background to three Japanese maples (*Acer*), and a Chinese lantern (*Physalis*) provides a central glow with its bright orange, lantern-shaped fruits. The irises bloom earlier in the year, but their leaves retain a sculptural quality.

Betula pendula
❀❀❀ ◊ ☼ ♉

Acer palmatum 'Garnet'
❀❀❀ ◊ ☼ ☼ ♉

Border basics

Size 8 x 8m (25 x 25ft)
Suits Woodland, large shrub border
Soil Well-drained, moist
Site Dappled shade

Shopping list

- 1 x *Betula pendula*
- 1 x *Acer palmatum* 'Garnet'
- 1 x *Acer palmatum* 'Bloodgood'
- 1 x *Acer palmatum* var. *dissectum* Dissectum Atropurpureum Group
- 3 x *Physalis alkekengi*
- 5 x Irises (bearded)

Physalis alkekengi
❀❀❀ ◊ ◊ ☼ ☼ ♉

Acer palmatum 'Bloodgood'
❀❀❀ ◊ ☼ ☼ ♉

Planting and aftercare

Avoid planting in windy, exposed sites, as the maple's delicate leaves will be shredded. Plant in autumn when the soil is warm, to give the trees time to establish before the onset of winter. Dig in leafmould to provide a friable soil structure for these woodland trees. Place the maples in a triangle with the smallest (Dissectum Atropurpureum) at the front, leaving about 3–4m (10–12ft) between each plant. If there is no existing woodland canopy, then plant the birch where it will provide some shade. The Chinese lantern should be planted between the maples and allowed to scramble among them. Plant perennials, such as these bearded irises, at the front, for flower colour earlier in the year and structural foliage from spring to autumn.

Acer palmatum var. *d.* Dissectum
Atropurpureum Group ❀❀❀ ◊ ☼

Iris (bearded)
❀❀❀ ◊ ☼

Winter woodland

This simple combination of one deciduous tree and three evergreen shrubs makes an attractive display throughout winter. The heather (*Erica*) covers the ground with its pink flowers, while the pine (*Pinus*) and holly (*Ilex*) give permanent structure. Hollies with variegated leaves are very decorative in the winter garden, and even more so if they have berries. The lovely cinnamon-coloured bark on the paper-bark maple (*Acer*) is eye-catching all year.

Border basics

Size 4 x 4m (12 x 12ft)
Suits Miniature woodland
Soil Light, well-drained
Site Sun or light shade

Shopping list

- 1 x *Acer griseum*
- 3 x *Erica carnea*
- 1 x *Ilex crenata* 'Variegata'
- 1 x *Pinus mugo*

Planting and aftercare

Remove the lower branches of the maple as it grows to form a single trunk that reveals more of its attractive bark.
This will also raise the canopy for shade-loving woodland shrubs, perennials, and bulbs to grow underneath. If rabbits are a problem, protect new plants with a guard around their trunks at the base. The heather tolerates most soil types and thrives in sun, so check your chosen site is not shaded by the other plants. This garden is low maintenance but weeds will need to be removed from time to time; cover the beds with a natural-looking mulch of bark, pine needles, or wood chippings. In spring, trim the heather to prevent it from going straggly, removing the old flowerheads and some of the foliage, and avoid cutting back into the old wood.

Acer griseum
❀❀❀ ◊ ◐ ☼ ◑ ♛

Erica carnea
❀❀❀ ◊ ☼

Ilex crenata 'Variegata'
❀❀❀ ◊ ◐ ☼

Pinus mugo
❀❀❀ ◊ ☼ ♛

Pruning basics

Pruning is quite easy once you have mastered the basic techniques outlined in this chapter. These should give you more confidence with your secateurs, but before you start pruning make sure you read the section on safety and legal issues. Then follow the advice on making essential cuts and how to remove a branch correctly. Also included is information on shaping trees and hedges, as well as step-by-step sequences showing how, through pruning, you can create exciting foliage displays, winter-stem interest, and topiary shapes.

Basic pruning techniques

Pruning is essential if you are to stay in control of your plants. Many have an optimum time for pruning, but often the best time is when you remember! Bear in mind that hard pruning can result in vigorous growth the following year.

Safety first To ensure that it's the plant and not you that looses a limb when pruning, an awareness of safety issues when wielding sharp implements is imperative.
Always wear gloves and eye protection These protect you from saws and secateurs, as well as thorns and spines. Ear defenders are needed when operating loud machinery. Stepladders should always be level and on solid ground. If possible, ask somebody wearing a hard hat to secure the ladder by standing on the bottom rung; never overstretch or lean over the side. Ensure that electrical equipment is plugged into an emergency circuit breaker and that the cable is kept behind the operator. Never use electrical equipment in wet weather. Never use a chainsaw without the appropriate training.
Finally – don't risk it! Thousands of people end up in hospital every year because of accidents in the garden. If a job looks too much to handle, call in the professionals.

Remove diseased branches Any diseased wood should be removed immediately before it has a chance to spread. If you are unsure whether or not a branch is dead, cut into it with secateurs. If it is fresh and springy inside, then it is still alive, although it could still be diseased.

Cut out crossing branches If the canopy is too dense, branches will cross, often rubbing together to cause long-term damage. Congested growth also reduces the amount of light reaching the stems, impeding flowering. Remove the least healthy stem by cutting back to a lower branch.

Prune to new growth Sometimes when wood is old or diseased it is important to cut back to new growth. This will also encourage new growth from or near the base of the plant. The overall effect is to invigorate the plant, provided that pruning is done with restraint.

Cutting alternate buds Make a slanting cut just above the bud, so raindrops trickle away from it. Usually you prune to an outward-facing bud to avoid shading at the centre, but floppy plants, like gooseberries, are pruned to an inward bud to keep them upright.

Cutting opposite buds On plants with buds opposite each other, such as maples and hydrangeas, make a straight cut just above a pair of buds. If too much of a stump is left, it may become diseased, but cutting too close may damage the bud, and it will fail to open.

Pinch pruning Often referred to as stopping, this involves removing the growing tip of a stem by pinching it off with your fingers. Pinch prune young, soft growth, and it will encourage sideshoots to grow. Use this method on "lollipop" trees to encourage a rounded, bushy head.

Removing branches This allows more light into the canopy and stimulates more productive growth. Use a sharp pruning saw to remove any branches that are thicker than a finger. Do not let the wood rip or tear, and avoid using loppers as they rarely make a clean cut.

Removing branches from trees and shrubs

To prune effectively, make sure you have the correct tools for the job, and keep all cutting equipment sharp and well maintained. If the job looks too much to handle, or branches are too high, contact a professional tree surgeon.

Right tools for the job Secateurs are used to prune stems smaller than 1.5cm (½in) in diameter. Slicing blades give a cleaner cut than anvil blades. Pruning saws can be used for branches thicker than a finger; avoid bow saws which are generally too cumbersome for pruning branches. Loppers are not ideal for pruning, as they don't cut as cleanly as a sharp saw, but you can use them for reducing the length of a branch before the final cut, or for chopping up prunings. Long-armed loppers and saws are useful for out-of-reach branches and usually come with interchangeable heads but, again, they don't make very clean cuts. They are a safer option than climbing a ladder, but always wear a hard hat and eye protection.

Torn branches Most branches are deceptively heavy and can tear easily if they aren't cut properly. Reduce them in sections with loppers to reduce the weight, then make the final cut with a pruning saw. If branches are too high or too large, call in a professional tree surgeon.

Bad cuts Never make pruning cuts flush to the trunk, as shown. The wound will struggle to heal properly, leaving it susceptible to disease and decay, which can eventually kill the tree. A large branch should be removed with an angled cut about 2–3cm (1in) away from the trunk.

Making a clean cut using the three-cut method

1 Identify the branch that needs to be removed. Try to remove growth when it is young, as the recovery is faster. Trees and shrubs will recover better from several small wounds, rather than one big one.

2 Make an undercut about 15cm (6in) away from the trunk, about half way through the branch. The second cut should be made from above, slightly further away from the trunk. This will remove the branch safely without tearing.

3 Remove the remaining branch stub with the third cut, starting from the upper surface of the branch, just beyond the crease in the bark where the branch meets the trunk. Angle the cut away from the trunk.

4 This pruning method results in a clean cut, and leaves the plant's healing tissue intact. The cut surface will soon begin to shrink as the tree produces protective bark, which will eventually cover the exposed area.

Renovating a shrub

Shrubs that have grown too big can either be cut down and replaced or hard pruned, like this smoke bush (*Cotinus*).

Not all plants respond well to such pruning. Many conifers, for example, will not regenerate from old wood.

1 Evaluate the shrub to be renovated in early spring, well before the main growing season. Drastic hard pruning is necessary to restore the shape of this shrub, to invigorate it, and to stop it from smothering nearby plants.

2 Remove any dead or diseased branches using a pruning saw. Then start to cut off the large branches, reducing their length in sections and remembering to make undercuts first to prevent torn branches (*see pp.90–91*).

3 Reduce the structure to just three or four branches from which the new stems will be produced. The height of the framework can be varied according to preference but about 60cm (24in) is ideal for keeping the plant compact.

4 Each year, remember to devote time to lightly pruning back the previous year's growth so that the shrub is kept within bounds. The plant will remain compact and the growth will be stronger and leaves more vibrant.

Pruning an early summer-flowering shrub

Most shrubs must be pruned annually if they are to perform at their best. Some need just a light trim, while others, like this mock orange (*Philadelphus*), are cut back harder to encourage new stems, which bear the most flowers, to form.

1 Wait until the flowers begin to fade before beginning to prune. With annual pruning, this mock orange will continue to bear its masses of scented white flowers in early summer year after year.

2 Cut back about a quarter of the oldest flowering stems to 15cm (6in) above the ground. This encourages young, vigorous stems to grow from the buds below the pruning cuts, and these will bear next year's flowers.

3 Shorten any old stems that have young growths lower down. Take off the top third of these old stems, pruning them back to a younger branch. Also remove any dead, damaged, or diseased wood.

4 Trim the tips of any strong young stems that are already present to encourage lower branching and more flowers. The finished plant should look more compact and tidy, and give rise to lots of young, fresh growth.

Pruning an apple tree

Annual pruning of apple trees will reward you with lots of blossom followed by an abundance of fruit. Prune in winter when you can clearly see the branch structure.

1 Prune apple trees gently to encourage the production of fruiting spur branches. This mature apple tree is in need of some renovation, and will benefit from pruning annually.

2 Remove some of the older upright branches that are blocking out the sun. Shade drastically reduces the amount of fruit that will be produced. Cut back these branches to the trunk (*see p.91*).

3 Use a secure and stable stepladder to reach the taller branches. Avoid using long-armed loppers or saws as it is difficult to make accurate and clean cuts from a distance.

4 Cut back either to a main branch or trunk, or to another branch of a similar size or slightly smaller. Do not leave a long stub, as it will die back and may become diseased.

Pruning an apple tree *continued*

5 Step back from the tree regularly and look at its overall shape. Try to free the centre of the tree from congestion and crossing branches, as well as any that are dead, damaged, or diseased.

6 Remove competing branches and thin out some of the short side branches (fruiting spurs). By removing this branch, the remaining spurs will receive more sunlight and be more productive.

7 Thin out young shoots as there is no room for them all to mature into fruiting branches. Leave about one or two young shoots to develop every 30cm (12in). Also remove any short or weak growths.

8 Work around the tree systematically to create a balanced framework with an open centre for good air circulation. Remove any branches growing at angles that distort the shape of the tree.

9 Prune with restraint as overpruned apple trees will react vigorously the following year. Such trees tend to grow lots of vegetative, leafy shoots with very few fruits or flowers.

Pruning fruit bushes

For any gardener with aspirations of home-grown fruit, pruning is an essential job. As well as removing dead and diseased branches, it improves the quality of fruit and retains the shape of the plant. It also allows sunlight and air into the canopy to ripen the fruit buds. Here are the pruning techniques for a selection of popular fruits.

Blueberries

To ensure a good crop, the first step is to plant more than one variety as this will improve pollination. After planting, blueberries can be left for three or four years to grow naturally, but after this the growth will become more congested and will need to be thinned if the plant is to remain productive. The fruit forms on wood that is produced the previous year, so pruning should be carried out in winter. Cut out one or two of the oldest stems at the base with loppers or a pruning saw. Dead or diseased wood also needs to be removed, as do any low-growing branches that will lie on the ground with the weight of summer fruit. If pine trees grow nearby, collect up their fallen needles and spread them around the base of the shrubs as a mulch for these acid soil-loving plants.

During winter, remove one or two of the oldest branches to ground level or to where a low sideshoot emerges.

Blueberries supply tasty and healthy super foods. They need acidic soil; many gardeners meet this need by growing them in pots.

At the same time of year, trim back any dead, diseased, damaged, or crossing growth, cutting back to a vigorous shoot.

Currants and Gooseberries

Gooseberries and redcurrants have similar growth habits. They both produce fruit on older wood and on the base of the new growth. They can be grown as open-centre goblets, fans, step-overs, or vertical cordons. The best method of growing them in a small space is as a vertical cordon as it means lots of different varieties can be grown against a fence or wall. To do this, train a central stem up a cane and tie it in each year until it eventually reaches about 1.8m (6ft). Each winter the new growth on all sideshoots should be pruned back to two buds. Blackcurrants are grown as shrubs and are planted deeper than redcurrants or gooseberries. They produce fruit on young canes and one-third of their older wood should be removed at ground level each winter.

Raspberries

There are two different types of raspberries: summer-fruiting and autumn-fruiting. Both types produce canes and should be trained along wires stretched between stout posts. Their fruiting habit is different and this needs to be understood in order to maximise fruit yields. Summer raspberries fruit on canes produced the year before. After fruiting in summer, cut down the old, fruited canes to ground level, then tie in only the healthiest of the new canes that have grown in the current growing season. They need to be spaced 6–10cm (2½–4in) apart. Autumn raspberries fruit on the canes produced that year; they should be left after fruiting and then all cut down to ground level in late winter or early spring. New canes will soon replace them; they do not need to be thinned.

Every winter, remove about one-third of the older wood of blackcurrants. Cut back to a strong shoot close to ground level.

At the end of the season, raspberries are a tangle of canes. For summer types, cut out all the old stems and tie in the new ones.

At the same time, remove completely any weak or thin stems, as well as any that are dead, damaged or diseased.

Hard prune autumn raspberries to ground level in late winter or early spring. New productive growth will soon follow.

Hedge trimming and pruning

All hedges need trimming and pruning to keep them in good shape. The base is usually wider than the top to allow light to reach the bottom, and the top can be flat, angled, or rounded, depending on your preference.

Informal hedge Perfect for romantic cottage gardens or wildlife areas, most informal hedges contain a variety of trees and shrubs. Although the look can be achieved with little work, clever plant selection and selective pruning in late summer is needed to ensure that an informal hedge keeps both its shape and "natural" appeal.

Tapering hornbeam hedge This shape gives better wind protection than a flat-topped hedge. Heavy snow will also slide off the top, preventing broken stems. Clipped hornbeams retain their dead leaves through winter, creating an effective year-round screen.

Formal yew hedge Distinct, formal evergreen shapes like this can only be achieved using plants with a very dense growth habit, such as yew, box, privet, or shrubby *Lonicera*. Yews are ideal as they grow fairly slowly, tolerate tight clipping, and regenerate if they need hard pruning.

Trimming a formal deciduous hedge Cut back in late summer, keeping the hedge trimmer flat to the hedge and moving it up and down in a sweeping movement. The electric cable must be fitted to a circuit breaker and kept behind you to prevent it from being cut.

Trimming a formal evergreen hedge Most types should be trimmed in late summer, although vigorous growers like Leyland cypress may need an additional cut earlier in the year. Box hedges should be cut once, in early summer, so that the regrowth has time to harden off.

Cutting a flat top Stretch string between stout posts on both sides of the hedge at the height required to give yourself two straight lines when pruning the top. Make sure that the string is kept taut and that the blades are horizontal so the cut is level.

Hedge renovation This might look drastic, but many overgrown trees and shrubs, such as hornbeam, respond well to hard pruning. It's best to tackle only the top and one side initially, as it gives the hedge a chance to recover before the other side is hard pruned the following year.

Pruning roses

Different types of roses have different pruning needs. Identify your roses and then follow these guidelines to ensure they produce their best show.

Old garden roses

These roses normally have one flush of flowers each year. Prune in early spring, first removing any dead, damaged, diseased, weak, and crossing branches. They do not need severe pruning; aim to reduce the size of the plant by one-third. Always make a sloping cut above an outward-facing bud. In the autumn, cut back the stems by one-third to reduce the risk of wind rocking the plant and damaging the roots.

Examples of old garden roses

- *Rosa* 'Blanche Double de Coubert'
- *Rosa* 'Boule de Neige'
- *Rosa* 'Charles de Mills'
- *Rosa* 'De Rescht'
- *Rosa* 'Fantin-Latour'
- *Rosa* 'Frau Dagmar Hartopp'
- *Rosa* 'Louise Odier'
- *Rosa* 'Madame Isaac Pereire'
- *Rosa* 'Madame Pierre Oger'
- *Rosa* 'Maiden's Blush'
- *Rosa mundi*
- *Rosa rugosa*
- *Rosa rugosa* 'Alba'
- *Rosa* 'Souvenir de la Malmaison'
- *Rosa* 'William Lobb'

Shrub roses

This group of roses normally flowers more than once during the summer months. They do not need hard pruning since they flower on older stems; the aim is to create a strong, uncluttered structure of mature wood. This improves air flow through the plant, which helps to prevent fungal diseases. In early spring, cut off any dead, damaged, weak, crossing, or diseased branches, then remove a few of the oldest stems down to the ground. Reduce healthy main stems by a quarter and prune some of their sideshoots by just a few centimetres. Always cut above a healthy bud that faces away from the centre of the plant, if possible. By midsummer, the plant should be covered in beautiful flowers. Remove dead flowerheads when they appear to encourage repeat flowering.

Examples of shrub roses

- *Rosa* 'Ballerina'
- *Rosa* Bonica
- *Rosa* 'Cerise Bouquet'
- *Rosa* 'Constance Spry'
- *Rosa* 'Dortmund'
- *Rosa* Eglantyne
- *Rosa* Falstaff
- *Rosa* 'Felicia'
- *Rosa* 'Fritz Nobis'
- *Rosa* Gertrude Jekyll
- *Rosa* Golden Celebration
- *Rosa* Graham Thomas
- *Rosa* 'Marguerite Hilling'
- *Rosa* 'Nevada'
- *Rosa* Rhapsody in Blue
- *Rosa* 'Sally Holmes'
- *Rosa* Sweet Juliet
- *Rosa xanthina* 'Canary Bird'

Hybrid tea roses

Like shrub roses, most hybrid teas are repeat-flowering. They bear their flowers singly or in small clusters and respond well to hard pruning in early spring. First remove all dead, damaged, diseased, weak, and crossing stems, and then prune out the oldest stems, taking them back to the ground. Leave between three and five young, strong stems, and prune these to a height of 15cm (6in) above the soil – about the same height as a pair of secateurs standing on end, which is a useful guide. Always make a sloping cut above an outward-facing bud, if possible. In summer, remove flowerheads as they fade to encourage further blooms. In late autumn or early winter, reduce the height of the stems by one-third to reduce the risk of wind rocking the plant and damaging the roots.

Examples of hybrid tea roses

- *Rosa* Alexander
- *Rosa* 'Blessings'
- *Rosa* Dawn Chorus
- *Rosa* 'Deep Secret'
- *Rosa* Elina
- *Rosa* Freedom
- *Rosa* Ingrid Bergman
- *Rosa* 'Just Joey'
- *Rosa* Lovely Lady
- *Rosa* Paul Shirville
- *Rosa* Peace
- *Rosa* Remember Me
- *Rosa* Savoy Hotel
- *Rosa* 'Silver Jubilee'
- *Rosa* Tequila Sunrise
- *Rosa* Troika
- *Rosa* Warm Wishes

Floribunda roses

These roses are well known for their many-headed clusters of blooms during the summer months. Pruning is very similar to hybrid tea roses, but not quite as hard. First, remove all dead, damaged, diseased, weak, and crossing stems. Your aim is to leave a framework of between six and eight of the strongest, youngest stems. Prune them to a height of between 20–30cm (8–12in), always making a sloping cut just above an outward-facing bud, if possible. Try to remove dead flowerheads as they appear through the summer to encourage repeat flowering, although this can be quite fiddly work with so many flowers. In late autumn or early winter, reduce the height of the stems by one-third to reduce the risk of damage when wind rocks the plant and disturbs its root system.

Examples of floribunda roses

- *Rosa* 'Arthur Bell'
- *Rosa* 'English Miss'
- *Rosa* Fascination
- *Rosa* Fellowship
- *Rosa* 'Fragrant Delight'
- *Rosa* Iceberg
- *Rosa* Memento
- *Rosa* Pretty Lady
- *Rosa* 'Princess of Wales'
- *Rosa* Queen Elizabeth
- *Rosa* Rememberance
- *Rosa* Sexy Rexy
- *Rosa* Sunset Boulevard
- *Rosa* Tall Story
- *Rosa* The Times Rose
- *Rosa* Trumpeter

Pruning for winter stems

Some dogwoods, willows, and *Rubus* are cut down almost to the ground each year to encourage masses of colourful young stems that provide a great winter display.

1 Remove all weak, dead, or diseased growth, reducing the congestion and improving access to the centre of the shrub. All winter-stem shrubs, like this dogwood (*Cornus*), should be pruned in late winter or early spring.

2 Cut back all the previous year's growth to the first pair of buds at the base of the stem. This will establish a system of young spurs, which will send out new stems.

3 Thin out some of the older, thicker spurs to reduce the chance of crossing stems that may rub and damage each other. Crossing growth will also make the plant look congested and untidy.

4 After pruning, you should be left with a simple, open structure from which a mass of strong, colourful new stems will grow. Add a mulch and a dressing of balanced slow-release fertilizer around the base of the plant.

Pruning for foliage effects

Foliage shrubs that tolerate hard pruning, like *Paulownia*, *Catalpa*, or variegated elder, can be cut each year to give wonderful displays of large, vibrant foliage at eye level.

Tip for success

Elder trees bear opposite buds, so prune straight across the branch, above the buds. Shrubs with alternate buds will need a sloping cut above the bud (*see p.89*).

1 Prune hard in early spring before the leaves start to emerge. The aim is to reduce the existing branches down to a low framework and invigorate the plant. Shown here is the variegated elder *Sambucus nigra* 'Aureomarginata'.

2 Reduce the stems of the previous year's growth back to two or three buds, using a sharp pair of loppers or, ideally, a pruning saw. Remove any weak or wispy stems completely, at the base.

3 Thin out some of the old, congested and dense wood from the centre of the plant using a pruning saw. Also remove any dead or diseased branches.

4 Leave a framework of branches about 75cm (30in) from the ground. Multiple stems will grow up to 2m (6ft) in one year. Mulch deeply around the base, leaving a space round the stems, and add a dressing of balanced fertilizer.

Making a topiary cone

Simple, architectural topiary shapes, such as cones, suit many situations, adding structure to formal borders and elegant terraces. They are also very easy to create.

Topiary tip

To prevent the spread of disease, sterilize your tools before trimming a new plant. Inexpensive household disinfectant will do the job. Rub on some oil after use, to prevent rust.

1 When buying box or other topiary plants, look for healthy specimens densely covered in unblemished leaves, with a strong leading upright shoot in the centre. Before planting, ensure that its "best" side is facing the front.

2 Stand above the plant, and locate a central shoot that will form the point at the top of the cone. With long-handled shears, start to trim the box from this point in an outward direction. Keep moving around the plant as you clip.

3 Stand back from time to time to assess the shape of the cone. To achieve a perfectly circular cone, look directly down at it from the central point. From this position you can see if the cone is clipped equally all around.

4 If your cone has a few gaps, don't be tempted to keep trimming, or you will end up with a tiny topiary. Leave the gaps, and after a few months young shoots will form and fill them out. Tidy up your cone twice a year in summer.

Caring for trees and shrubs

Keep your trees and shrubs looking good all year round by following the advice here on general maintenance, such as weeding and feeding. Also improve the health of your plants by watering efficiently – and help to conserve valuable water resources. Find out, too, what pests and diseases may attack your precious plants, and discover the best way of moving a tree or shrub if it's in the wrong position.

Watering and mulching

For the first few years after planting trees and shrubs, water them regularly. Once established, they should look after themselves – if you chose and planted them well in the first place.

What to water Direct water onto the soil over the roots, not onto the leaves. A saucer-shaped dip around the main stem creates a reservoir while water soaks down to the roots. Failure to water sufficiently after planting, especially during dry periods, will compromise growth and may kill the plant. If it is still struggling and wilting after three years, then something serious is wrong; consider replacing it with a plant more suitable to the conditions. Plants in containers will need frequent watering, probably every day during the summer. A thick layer of mulch over the soil will conserve moisture by reducing evaporation.

Wise ways to water

Choose plants that can cope with drought, if this is likely to be a problem, and don't water mature trees and shrubs. Lay seep hoses as they provide a steady flow of water to where it is needed, and water in the evening or early morning when less will evaporate. No matter how small your garden, there should be room for at least one water butt. These containers catch and store rainwater, which is ideal for watering plants; they may also save you money if your water supply is metered. Add organic matter to the soil as it helps to retain moisture.

Create a dip around new plants by mounding up the soil to channel the water down to the roots and to prevent it running away.

Seep hoses are very efficient, as the water drips directly around the root area, and very little is lost through splashing or evaporation.

Why use a mulch? Firstly, mulches help to seal in soil moisture, thereby reducing evaporation and water loss. Mulches made from organic matter act like a sponge, absorbing the moisture from rain and the air and then slowly releasing it to the plant roots below. Secondly, as an organic mulch slowly rots, it is taken down towards the roots by worms and the rain, improving the soil structure. Thirdly, a mulch will suppress weeds by excluding light from the soil surface and hindering their development. This only tends to work if the mulch is sterile, which is usually true for shop-bought mulches, but home-made garden compost may contain weed seeds. As the surface of a newly laid mulch is quite loose, however, it is quite easy to destroy emergent weeds by shallow hoeing. Also remember to keep organic mulches away from shrub and tree stems, as the moisture they retain can rot the wood.

Spread a thick mulch around the base of a tree or shrub to a depth of 5–15cm (2–6in). Reapply every one to three years.

Mulching materials

Wood chip or bark is the favourite choice for tree and shrub borders as it blends in with the surroundings. Weeds cannot easily germinate in it, and as it is slow to rot down it needs to be replenished less frequently than compost or manure. Gravel is a popular mulch for rock gardens, Japanese designs, Mediterranean and herb gardens. It is a good idea to lay landscape fabric, such as woven polypropylene, under gravel. This is permeable to water yet impermeable to weeds, but fabric is unsightly, so it needs covering with a loose mulch.

Gravel is an effective mulch but will gradually mix into the soil if landscape fabric is not laid underneath it.

Spread a mulch so that it covers the ground under the tree or shrub canopy. Push it under any low-lying branches.

Weeding and feeding

For a beautiful garden, you must remember to weed and feed. Weeds compete with your plants for nutrients and moisture in the soil, while fertilizers promote healthy and strong growth.

Weeds should be removed as quickly and as thoroughly as possible to prevent them from germinating and spreading.

Why weed? Not only can weeds look unsightly, but they also compete with trees and shrubs for three vital resources: water, light, and nutrients. It is worth bearing in mind, however, that a weed is just a plant growing in the wrong place. If you can tolerate a few weeds in out-of-the-way places, the wildlife will thank you for it.

Weeding methods The most effective method of weed control is to cover the soil with plants. Ground-cover shrubs are ideal for this purpose and leafy tree canopies reduce the amount of light and moisture needed by most weeds. Other areas of bare soil should be covered with a mulch (see p.112). Hand weeding is the simplest method of control, and the most effective weeding tool is the border fork. Hoeing is useful for removing weeds on bare patches of ground, but it can damage surface roots if you hoe too close to trees and shrubs. Annual weeds can be simply pulled out before they have a chance to set seed, but perennial weeds need tougher action. Either treat them with a weedkiller or dig out the roots meticulously. Avoid using a rotavator to clear ground as all it will do is chop up perennial weeds into tiny pieces, multiplying them by hundreds of times.

Hoeing can effectively control annual weeds, but be careful not to damage the shallow roots of trees and shrubs.

Perennial weeds can regrow from a tiny piece of stem or root. Dry them in the sun to destroy them; don't add to the compost heap.

Using weedkillers Herbicides can be very effective, particularly if you have a large area of perennial weeds to tackle. They can be bought either ready mixed as a spray or as a concentrated liquid that requires diluting and applying with a watering can or knapsack sprayer. Always wear the appropriate protective clothing as recommended on the label and closely follow the manufacturer's instructions and rate of application. Take care not to get herbicide on yourself or any ornamental plants growing nearby; for this reason it is always good practice to apply herbicides on still, windless days. Systemic weedkillers, usually containing the active ingredient glyphosate, are effective on perennial weeds as they absorb the chemical and take it down into the roots. Contact weedkillers burn off the leaves and stems but won't kill the roots. They are suitable for annual weeds only.

Choosing plant foods Fertilizers are plant foods containing essential nutrients. Most are supplied in a concentrated form and contain the three major nutrients essential for plant growth, in varying ratios: nitrogen (N), phosphorus (P), and potassium or potash (K). Look for the N:P:K ratio on the packet. Nitrogen encourages vegetative growth, phosphorus promotes healthy roots, and potash helps flowering and fruiting. General-purpose fertilizers contain these nutrients in almost equal amounts and can be applied to the soil prior to planting or as a general feed to keep plants healthy. Rose feeds are high in potash; they are also suitable for all established trees and shrubs that are grown for their flowers or fruit. Organic fertilizers include dried bone, bonemeal, hoof and horn, and seaweed. Controlled-release fertilizers are generally only used at planting time or for container plants.

Yellowing between the veins of the leaves, often seen on acid-loving plants, is a sign of manganese or iron deficiency in the soil.

When and how to apply plant food Most established trees and shrubs require no feeding. When they do, use a foliar spray applied onto the leaves, as it is the most effective method. Plants in containers benefit from a general feed every week during the growing season. Give sickly looking specimens a general feed in spring. Avoid feeding plants after midsummer as this stimulates growth that will not have time to ripen prior to winter, which may then be damaged by frost. Fertilizers usually come in granular form or as a concentrated liquid, which requires mixing with water. Wear gloves when handling all forms of fertilizer, and always follow the manufacturer's instructions, applying them at the recommended rates. Don't feed plants if heavy rain is forecast, as the nutrients may be washed away, or under the midday sun on hot days; plants fed at this time can suffer from sun scorch.

Measure quantities correctly when using fertilizers and do not overfeed. These chemicals are toxic to plants in high concentrations.

Soluble granular fertilizers provide instant nutrition; dilute according to the instructions on the pack, and apply to the soil.

Quick fixes for sickly plants Trees and shrubs may need a quick pick-me-up if they start to look unhealthy. Pale green leaves and weak, poor growth is often due to a lack of nitrogen. This requires a high-nitrogen fertilizer to remedy the problem, such as sulphate of ammonia. Dried blood can also be used. Brown discoloration or blotches on the leaves, leaf margins, or leaf tips is usually a sign of a potassium deficiency. Apply a high-potash solution, such as tomato feed or sulphate of potash. Stunted growth and pale leaves could be phosphate deficiency; apply bone meal or superphosphate. Yellowing between the veins is commonly seen on acid-loving plants, such as rhododendrons and camellias. It is caused by manganese or iron deficiency, where an alkaline soil prevents these nutrients from being absorbed. Builders rubble and mortar can be culprits. Treat with sequestered iron.

Winter care

A quiet time in the gardener's calendar, winter is the traditional season to check over your woody plants. Those that are not fully hardy will either need to be moved indoors or wrapped up.

Maintenance tasks Now the branches of deciduous trees are bare, it is easier to check for dead, crossing, damaged, or diseased branches. Remove these before spring, employing a tree surgeon for any large jobs. Check around the base of the main stems for pest damage and ensure that stakes are secure, loosening any tree ties if they are too tight. Rake up the leaves from paths and lawns. Remove any that are smothering small shrubs, as they will cause the plants to rot. If you have a lot of fallen leaves, it is worth making a "leaf bin", where they will rot down to create useful leafmould. Take a look at your garden and decide whether any trees and shrubs need to be added, removed, reduced, or rejuvenated.

To protect the growing tips of tree ferns and palms, wrap up their heads over winter. The leaves may die back, but they will resprout.

Plants that need winter protection Ideally, only choose plants that will thrive in the given climate and conditions. However, there are many frost-tender or borderline hardy woody plants that are good to grow, some of which are listed below. Just before winter, move tender plants in containers under cover, such as into a greenhouse, porch, or conservatory. Trees and shrubs that cannot be moved will need to be covered up with hessian, fleece, straw, leaves, or even bubble plastic to keep them warm. Some plants will die or be seriously damaged if not protected over winter. Others, like peaches and apricots, are fully hardy but have spring flowers or young shoots that are prone to frost. These plants will need covering up overnight when spring frosts are forecast.

- *Abelia floribunda*
- *Abutilon* 'Kentish Belle'
- *Acacia dealbata*
- *Agave americana*
- *Araucaria heterophylla*
- *Bougainvillea*
- *Brugmansia*
- *Brunfelsia pauciflora*
- *Butia capitata*
- *Callistemon citrinus*
- *Carpenteria californica*
- *Cyathea dealbata*
- *Dicksonia antarctica*
- *Fremontodendron*
- *Hibiscus rosa-sinensis*
- *Melianthus major*
- *Musa basjoo*
- *Myrtus communis*
- *Olea europaea*
- Peaches and apricots
- *Pittosporum tenuifolium*
- *Plumbago auriculata*
- *Plumeria rubra*
- *Ricinus communis*
- *Senecio cineraria*
- *Tibouchina urvilleana*

Overwintering frost-tender plants

1 Push four bamboo canes into the ground around the plant and attach chicken wire to form a cage. Do this in advance of the first frosts. Banana trees (*Musa*), shown above, will need their top growth removed.

2 Pack dry straw into the wire cage and push it right down between the stems onto the crown of the plant. Dry bracken or leaves can be used as an alternative to straw.

Tender fruits

3 Stretch plastic sheeting over the bundle and tie it to the bamboo canes. This keeps the plant dry and prevents rotting; remove plastic on warm days to prevent plants sweating. Use bubble plastic if extra insulation is required.

Protect the blossom of slightly tender, wall-trained fruit trees, such as peaches, nectarines, or apricots, by rolling horticultural fleece down over the plant when frosts are forecast. The fleece should be rolled back up in the morning if the temperatures have lifted.

Moving a poorly positioned tree or shrub

Occasionally it is necessary to move a tree or shrub. It may have outgrown its position or you may simply want to take it with you when you move house. Unless the job is urgent, it's best to wait until the plant is dormant in winter.

1 Clear the ground around the plant to allow for easy access and digging. Choose a dry, mild day when the soil is workable, rather than attempting to dig into ground that is waterlogged or frozen.

2 Prepare the new hole in advance so that the plant can be moved to its new position swiftly. Clear the area of weeds and make a circular hole large and deep enough to take the transplant (*see also p.39*).

3 Carefully dig around the plant with a spade, trying to include as many of the roots as possible. As a rule of thumb, the roots should be as wide as the outer edge of the plant's canopy.

4   Lift the plant out of the hole and wrap the roots up, ideally in wet hessian, but an old gardening bag or blanket will do. The idea is to prevent the roots from drying out, so transfer the plant to its new hole as soon as possible.

5   Place the plant in the new hole and use a cane to check the planting depth. Make sure that the tree is planted no deeper than before, adding or taking away soil from the bottom of the hole as necessary.

6   Water the transplant in well and repeat through the following spring and summer. Apply a mulch to help retain moisture. If any branches die back after the move, prune them back to healthy wood. Keep the site free of weeds.

Dealing with pests

Controlling pests is a contentious issue. Many people confront them with chemicals; others encourage all wildlife into the garden, whether they are pests or not, which can increase biodiversity and help to create a natural balance.

Deterring pests Regardless of which camp you fall into prevention is always better than cure, and there are many cultivation techniques that reduce pest damage. Always check plants thoroughly before purchasing so you do not introduce pests into your garden; look after your plants well so they grow strongly and are able to resist attack; choose varieties that are resistant to pests and diseases; and regularly check your plants for infestations or symptoms of damage, like holes in leaves, before it is too late to act. If you do discover pests, consider picking them off by hand rather than immediately reaching for the spray gun, since some pesticides also kill off beneficial bugs, such as bees and ladybirds and their larvae.

Barriers against mammals Rabbits are common pests, but there are several mammals that can destroy trees and shrubs by gnawing bark and young shoots and digging at roots. Protect individual plants with plastic or wire guards around the base of the trunk or main stems. Use wire fencing around the garden to exclude larger mammals.

Counter attack The larvae of ladybirds, hoverflies, and lacewings are your friends, as they feed on pests like aphids, so encourage them into the garden. Other biological controls, such as nematodes for vine weevil, can be bought by mail order.

Check regularly Be vigilant for pests so that you can nip them in the bud before they multiply and get out of control. Remember to look not just for the pest, but also for symptoms, such as sick-looking plants, damage to leaves, and distorted growing tips.

Using chemicals Pesticides should only be used as a last resort, when there are serious infestations that threaten the life of a plant. Always follow the manufacturer's instructions carefully and wear rubber gloves when diluting or applying pesticides.

Common pests and how to control them

Woolly beech aphid Fluffy white patches appear on the leaves and shoot tips in early summer. Foliage becomes sticky and blackened with sooty mould. Spray with imidacloprid.

Vine weevils Adults eat notches in the leaf margins, but most damage is caused by the root-feeding larvae (*see top*). Drench the compost with pathogenic nematodes or treat plants in containers with thiacloprid.

Sawflies Most sawfly larvae feed openly, and strip leaves off plants. The rose leaf-rolling sawfly larvae feed inside rolled leaves. Pick off the caterpillar-like larvae, or spray with bifenthrin or pyrethrum pesticides.

Scale insects Shell-like bumps appear on stems and the undersides of leaves, which can result in poor growth. Some species excrete a sticky liquid called honeydew, encouraging sooty moulds. Spray with imidacloprid, plant oils, or fatty acids.

Capsid bugs Feeding from shoot tips and buds, these sap suckers cause many small holes in leaves that are near growing tips. On apple trees, the fruits have raised corky scabs. Spray with bifenthrin pesticide as soon as damage is seen.

Deer These gnaw bark and shoots and trample young plants. Repellent sprays and scaring devices have limited effectiveness. To keep deer out you need expensive fencing up to 1.8m (6ft) high, or large tree guards that prevent them leaning over.

Dealing with pests *continued*

Common pests and how to control them

Viburnum beetles Mainly found on *Viburnum opulus* and *V. tinus*. The larvae and adults eat holes in the foliage. Spray with bifenthrin or thiacloprid pesticides when damage starts in spring.

Pieris lacebugs A sap-feeding pest that causes yellowish mottling and bronzing on the leaves. Spray with bifenthrin or imidacloprid pesticides against the newly hatched nymphs in late spring.

Rosemary beetles Adults and larvae eat the foliage and flowers of lavender, rosemary, thyme, and sage. Adults look like metallic ladybirds. Remove them by hand when seen or spray with thiacloprid pesticide.

Bay sucker Leaf margins on bay trees curl, thicken, and turn yellow then brown. Prune or pick off affected leaves and shoots or spray with thiacloprid. The adults are small, greenish-brown winged insects.

Box sucker Causes stunted new shoots and cupped leaves with waxy white marks. In spring, pale green, wingless nymphs are seen on shoot tips. Control is generally unnecessary, especially on plants that are clipped.

Holly leaf miner Yellow or brown blotches appear on the leaves of holly trees and bushes. These marks may be unsightly, but no real harm is done. There are no effective control measures.

Horse chestnut leaf miner A new pest that causes whitish-brown mines between the leaf veins. Early leaf fall and slow growth are symptoms. Burn all fallen leaves to destroy the over-wintering pupae.

Rhododendron leafhoppers Buds turn brown and fail to open. Caused by leafhoppers laying eggs in the flower buds. Remove and burn affected buds; spray with bifenthrin or imidacloprid in late summer.

Winter moths Caterpillars nibble young growth and blossom. A grease band around the trunk in autumn stops the wingless females climbing the plant. Spray small trees with bifenthrin as leaves emerge in spring.

Adelgids Small, sap-feeding, aphid-like insects that feed on the needles, stems, or bark of some conifers. Little significant damage is done on established trees, so these pests can be tolerated or brushed off.

Gall mites Symptoms include a range of disfigurements, such as raised pouches, rolled leaf margins, enlarged buds, and hairy leaves. The damage is usually minimal and must be tolerated as there is no control.

Gall wasps Most gall wasps feed on oak trees, causing deformities on the leaves, buds, catkins, acorns, and roots. They should be tolerated as no serious damage occurs and control measures are impractical.

Diseases and disorders

When a bacterium, fungus, or virus attacks a plant it becomes diseased and may even die. Trees and shrubs are most vulnerable when young, just after planting, but once established they stand a much better chance of survival.

Preventative care Plants of even the most experienced gardener can succumb to disease, but a little common sense and gardening knowledge will increase their chances of survival. When buying, avoid plants that look sickly, stressed, or weak, and give preference to disease-resistant varieties. Keep new and susceptible plants well watered during periods of drought and watch out for early signs of disease, removing or spraying infected tissue before it can spread. Hard pruning is a useful remedy – for some plants only – as it removes the infection, encourages vigorous regrowth, and increases air circulation. Pruning at the wrong time of year can promote infection; cherry trees, for example, must be pruned in the summer only.

The best start in life When buying, always match a plant to its growing environment, and take time to plant it well. Remember also to care for the plant in its formative years by nourishing the soil. A plant's risk of disease is greatly reduced if it's planted in the correct surroundings, at the right depth, and with suitable sun and soil.

Using chemicals The height and size of many trees and shrubs make the application of chemical treatments impractical, but they have their uses on younger plants or on valuable specimens that are suffering badly and will be lost if action is not taken immediately. Always read the label, following the manufacturer's instructions carefully, and wear the recommended protective clothing.

Disease or disorder? Unlike diseases, "disorders" are caused by inappropriate growing conditions, leading to problems like leaf discoloration, stem distortions, or wilting. Causes include too much sun or shade, erratic watering, inadequate soil conditions, weedkiller damage, and frost. There is no real cure except to check on a plant's growing requirements and to try and improve conditions.

Common diseases and how to treat them

Powdery mildew White powdery patches appear on the leaves, usually during dry conditions. Water the plant at the first sign of disease and spray with a fungicide, or remove infected shoots as they appear.

Canker Branches and trunks develop depressions, cracks, and darker wood that can eventually kill the plant. There is no effective cure, particularly if it occurs in the trunk; removing affected branches will reduce the problem.

Coral spot Distinctive raised bright orange spots appear on dying wood. This is often caused by not correctly pruning to a bud, resulting in the tissue dying back. Remove the infected wood immediately and burn.

Honey fungus White fungal growth under the bark towards the base of the tree, toadstools in autumn, and black "bootlace" strands below the soil indicate the presence of this killer. Remove infected plants, including all their roots, immediately.

Black spot Black patches appear on the leaves of roses during summer. The problem is usually worse in warm, humid conditions. Pick off affected foliage and treat serious infections with a fungicide. When buying, select resistant varieties.

Rust Commonly seen on many trees and shrubs, particularly during humid conditions, rust is recognizable by raised browny-orange spots on the leaves. It can be treated by spraying with a fungicide or removing infected plant material.

Plant guide

This guide includes the most reliable, attractive, and popular trees and shrubs to help you to select the best for your garden. Plants are divided into trees, large shrubs, medium-sized shrubs and small shrubs, although sizes can vary depending on your site and soil. The symbols below are used to indicate the conditions each plant requires.

Key to plant symbols

   ♈   Plants given the RHS Award of Garden Merit

Soil preference

   ●   Well-drained soil

   ◐   Moist soil

   ○   Wet soil

Preference for sun or shade

   ☀   Full sun

   ◑   Partial or dappled shade

   ○   Full shade

Hardiness ratings

   ✳✳✳   Fully hardy plants

   ✳✳   Plants that survive outside in mild regions or sheltered sites

   ✳   Plants that need protection from frost over winter

Trees

Acer capillipes
The snake bark maple is a stunning tree. Its attractive, stripy green and grey bark and unusual arching and spreading habit offers year-round interest. The three-lobed leaves turn a spectacular orange and red in autumn.

H: 10m (30ft); **S**: 10m (30ft)
❄❄❄ ◊ ☼ ☼ ☼ ♛

Acer davidii
David's maple is a small tree also known as snake bark maple due to its stripy green and white bark. It can be grown with a single trunk, but is often grown multi-stemmed. Popular cultivars include 'George Forrest', 'Ernest Wilson', and 'Serpentine'.

H: 15m (50ft); **S**: 15m (50ft)
❄❄❄ ◊ ☼ ☼

Acer griseum
The paper bark maple is a spectacular tree that provides impressive winter interest with its thin, peeling bark with cinnamon-coloured undercoat. The autumn leaves are a gorgeous scarlet. To truly enjoy the flaking trunk, remove the lower branches.

H: 10m (30ft); **S**: 10m (30ft)
❄❄❄ ◊ ☼ ☼ ☼ ♛

Acer japonicum *'Aconitifolium'*
Forming a wide-spreading tree or bush, this maple deserves pride of place in any garden for its green, deeply lobed, toothed leaves that turn ruby red in autumn. It has small red flowers in spring followed by red-tinted, winged fruits.

H: 5m (15ft); **S**: 6m (20ft)
❄❄❄ ◊ ☼ ☼ ☼ ♛

Acer palmatum *var.* dissectum *Dissectum Atropurpureum Group*
Due to this maple's dwarf, shrubby habit, it is ideal for small gardens in a place sheltered from harsh winds. It also grows well in large containers, if kept well watered. The purple foliage is delicate and intricate.

H: 2m (6ft); **S**: 3m (10ft)
❄❄❄ ◊ ☼

Acer palmatum *'Sango-kaku'*
This popular tree with an elegant, upright habit is often known as the coral bark maple due to the orange-red colour of its branches and trunk, particularly noticeable in winter. In autumn the lobed leaves turn golden yellow. Sometimes called 'Senkaki'.

H: 6m (20ft); **S**: 5m (15ft)
❄❄❄ ◊ ☼ ☼ ☼ ♛

Betula nigra

The attractive peeling bark, which improves as it matures, is a particular feature of this medium-sized birch. Impressive yellow-brown catkins dangle from the branches in spring, and the diamond-shaped leaves turn buttery yellow in autumn.

H: 18m (60ft); **S**: 12m (40ft)
❋❋❋ ◊ ☼

Betula utilis *var.* jacquemontii

The smooth, peeling white bark of this birch makes a bold feature whether planted as a group or as a single specimen. The leaves turn golden yellow in autumn. 'Silver Shadow' is a particularly good cultivar with one of the purest white trunks.

H: 18m (60ft); **S**: 10m (30ft)
❋❋❋ ◊ ☼ ☀ ♆

Cercis canadensis *'Forest Pansy'*

A multi-stemmed tree with attractive purple, heart-shaped leaves that feel velvety to the touch. Pink, pea-shaped flowers appear before the leaves in spring. Impressive as a single specimen but also useful for the back of the border.

H: 10m (30ft); **S**: 10m (30ft)
❋❋❋ ◊ ☼ ☀ ♆

Cercis siliquastrum

The Judas tree is deciduous and bushy and produces rose-coloured, pea-shaped flowers in spring, followed by attractive purple-tinted seedpods. Although hardy it originates from the Mediterranean, so avoid very cold sites for best results.

H: 10m (30ft); **S**: 10m (30ft)
❋❋❋ ◊ ☼ ☀ ♆

Chamaecyparis obtusa *'Nana Gracilis'*

A slow-growing, dwarf conifer, this tree has a dense, pyramidal shape with glossy green, aromatic sprays of foliage and small brown cones. It's an ideal choice for small gardens, rockeries, or large containers.

H: 3m (10ft); **S**: 3m (10ft)
❋❋❋ ◊ ☼

Cordyline australis

With its palm-like foliage this is an ideal tree for creating a subtropical theme to a garden. It can be grown in a container in cooler areas and moved under cover in winter. Variegated forms are popular, such as 'Sundance' and 'Torbay Dazzler'.

H: 3–10m (10–30ft); **S**: 1–4m (3–12ft)
❋❋ ◊ ☼ ♆

Trees

Cornus kousa *'Satomi'*

A stunning flowering dogwood that offers something for every season. In autumn the leaves turn fiery red and orange, and large, deep-pink, star-shaped bracts appear in late spring. It also has strawberry-like fruits in late summer that persist into winter.

H: 7m (22ft); **S**: 5m (15ft)
❀❀❀ ◊ ☼ ☀ ♈

Cornus mas

The Cornelian cherry is a small, spreading tree, which is at its most impressive in winter when clusters of yellow flowers smother the bare branches. The leaves turn a fine red-purple in autumn, alongside the display of small, cherry-like fruits.

H: 5m (15ft); **S**: 5m (15ft)
❀❀❀ ◊ ☼ ☀

Corylus avellana *'Contorta'*

The corkscrew hazel is a slow-growing, deciduous shrub that is at its most striking in winter when its curious habit of contorted, twisted branches can be seen most clearly. Yellow catkins appear in late winter. The stems cut well for indoor display.

H: 5m (15ft); **S**: 5m (15ft)
❀❀❀ ◊ ☼ ☀

Corylus maxima *'Purpurea'*

The purple hazel offers attractive foliage to the gardener. Interesting red-purple catkins are produced on bare stems in late winter. Cut the stems down to near ground level in winter to contain its size and to create a bushier shape.

H: 6m (20ft); **S**: 5m (15ft)
❀❀❀ ◊ ☼ ☀ ♈

Crataegus laevigata *'Paul's Scarlet'*

One of the most popular ornamental hawthorns in cultivation, this small, round-headed deciduous tree is grown for its double pink spring flowers. Due to its sharp thorns, avoid in gardens with small children.

H: to 8m (25ft); **S**: to 8m (25ft)
❀❀❀ ◊ ☼ ☀ ♈

Dicksonia antarctica

Tree ferns have become enormously popular over the last few years, and none more so than this species. The fronds unfurl in spring from the top of the mass of fibrous roots that form the trunk. In cold winters, protect the crown with a wrapping of straw.

H: 3m (10ft) or more; **S**: 4m (12ft)
❀❀ ◊ ◊ ☀ ☀ ♈

Gleditsia triacanthos *'Sunburst'*

The honey locust is a fast-growing, handsome deciduous tree capable of tolerating pollution and drought. This form is grown for its delicate, finely divided foliage which is golden-yellow when young. It is a thornless tree with long seed pods.

H: 12m (40ft); **S**: 10m (30ft)
❄❄❄ ◊ ☼ ⚱

Laburnum *x* watereri *'Vossii'*

With its golden yellow, dangling chains of flowers up to 60cm (24in) in length, this spreading, deciduous tree makes an impressive feature. It can tolerate poor and shallow soil. Warning: all parts of this plant are very poisonous.

H: 8m (25ft); **S**: 8m (25ft)
❄❄❄ ◊ ☼ ⚱

Laurus nobilis

Cooks adore bay trees because of their aromatic, evergreen leaves. Although it can be grown as a tree, it can also be trained into formal shapes or standards by clipping regularly with secateurs. The flowers, and berries that follow, are insignificant.

H: 12m (40ft); **S**: 10m (30ft)
❄❄❄ ◑ ◊ ☼ ◑ ⚱

Ligustrum lucidum

Fragrant white flowers cover the Chinese privet tree in late summer, followed by blackish-blue berries in autumn. With its large, glossy, evergreen leaves, it makes an attractive, dense hedge tolerant of poor soils and city pollution.

H: 10m (30ft); **S**: 10m (30ft)
❄❄❄ ◑ ◊ ☼ ◑ ⚱

Magnolia liliiflora *'Nigra'*

An ideal tree for a small garden, this compact, deciduous magnolia bears large, goblet-shaped, deep red-purple flowers during late spring. Preferring neutral to acidic soil, the advantage of this tree over other magnolias is its ability to flower from a young age.

H: 3m (10ft); **S**: 2.5m (8ft)
❄❄❄ ◑ ◊ ☼ ◑ ⚱

Magnolia stellata

Star magnolia is one of the most popular and smallest spring-flowering magnolias, named for its white, star-shaped blooms. These emerge before the leaves and are vulnerable to spring frost, particularly if hit by early morning sunshine.

H: 3m (10ft); **S**: 4m (12ft)
❄❄❄ ◑ ◊ ☼ ◑ ⚱

Trees

Malus *'John Downie'*

A deciduous, ornamental apple tree producing stunning white blossom in spring, ideal for pollinating other apple trees in the garden. The crab apples are bright orange and red in autumn and make a superb crab-apple jelly. Attractive to wildlife.

H: 10m (30ft); **S**: 6m (20ft)
❄❄❄ ◊ ◖ ☼ ◑ ☼ ♈

Malus *x zumi 'Golden Hornet'*

A profusion of attractive yellow fruits in autumn makes this a favourite with both gardeners and wildlife. This tree is also an excellent pollinator for neighbouring apple trees due to the abundance of white blossom flushed with pink in spring.

H: 10m (30ft); **S**: 8m (25ft)
❄❄❄ ◊ ◖ ☼ ◑ ☼ ♈

Nyssa sinensis

The deciduous leaves on the Chinese tupelo display a wide array of autumn colours from mellow yellows to fiery oranges and reds. It prefers acidic soil. The green-grey bark takes on an interesting flaky texture as it matures. N. sylvatica is also popular, but larger.

H: 10m (30ft); **S**: 10m (30ft)
❄❄❄ ◖ ☼ ◑ ☼ ♈

Olea europaea

The olive tree has attractive silvery foliage and small white flowers in summer. It requires a warm, sheltered position, or plant it in a container and move under glass in winter. When mature the old, knarled trunk is an additional feature.

H: 10m (30ft); **S**: 10m (30ft)
❄❄ ◊ ☼

Picea glauca *'Conica'*

A dwarf conifer with a neat, dense, conical habit that makes a good specimen for a rock garden. It prefers slightly acidic soil. In spring the young needles are an attractive light green, and new cones are green during summer and later ripen to brown.

H: 2–6m (6–20ft); **S**: 1–2.5m (3–8ft)
❄❄❄ ◖ ☼

Pinus mugo *'Mops'*

This very dwarf pine with a spherical shape is ideal for a miniature rock garden or small container on a patio or balcony. It also makes an attractive feature when planted in large groups because of its round habit. It grows very slowly.

H: 1m (3ft); **S**: 1m (3ft)
❄❄❄ ◊ ☼ ♈

Prunus dulcis

Almond trees are grown for both their lavish display of pale pink blossom in spring and their pointed, oval nuts in summer, which require a warm site to ripen. 'Alba' has white flowers, and 'Macrocarpa' has larger flowers and nuts.

H: 8m (25ft); **S**: 8m (25ft)
❄❄❄ ◊ ◖ ☼

Prunus rufa

This ornamental cherry is grown for its stunning, glossy, deep red stems with horizontal tan-coloured stripes and peeling bark. It is a good smaller alternative to P. serrula for creating a dramatic feature in a winter garden. The spring blossom is pale pink.

H: 6m (20ft); **S**: 6m (20ft)
❄❄❄ ◊ ◖ ☼

Prunus serrula

Grown for its bark rather than its flowers, this deciduous ornamental cherry has dramatic peeling, reddish-brown bark with a polished sheen and pale horizontal stripes. The white blossom is followed by small red cherries dangling from long stalks.

H: 10m (30ft); **S**: 10m (30ft)
❄❄❄ ◊ ◖ ☼ ♉

Prunus 'Shôgetsu'

This tree is considered to be one of the best Japanese flowering cherries. The attractive pink buds are followed by long clusters of large white many-petalled flowers. Keep pruning to a minimum, in spring or summer only, to reduce the risk of infection.

H: 5m (15ft); **S**: 8m (25ft)
❄❄❄ ◊ ◖ ☼ ♉

Pyrus salicifolia 'Pendula'

This delightful ornamental pear tree has an elegant weeping habit with silvery-grey, willow-like leaves. An abundant show of creamy-white flowers in spring is followed by small, hard, brownish-green, inedible pears in late summer.

H: 5m (15ft); **S**: 4m (12ft)
❄❄❄ ◊ ☼ ♉

Robinia pseudoacacia 'Frisia'

Creating a splash of golden yellow with its attractive foliage, this tree makes a superb focal point. It can become large, but with regular hard-pruning it can be grown as a smaller, multi-stemmed tree. Clusters of white flowers sometimes appear in summer.

H: up to 15m (50ft); **S**: 8m (25ft)
❄❄❄ ◊ ◖ ☼ ♉

Trees

Salix babylonica *'Tortuosa'*

The curiously contorted branches of this willow are good for winter show, and they can be encouraged by hard pruning in late winter. This also keeps the tree to size. Other features include attractive yellow catkins, curly leaves, and purplish new shoots.

H: to 15m (50ft); **S**: to 8m (25ft)
❄❄❄ ◐ ☼ ♈

Salix caprea *'Kilmarnock'*

This elegant weeping willow is small enough to fit into most gardens. It is grown for its abundance of silver catkins that cover the tree in spring, before the leaves come out. Thin out the congested branches in winter to help maintain its graceful shape.

H: 1.5–2m (5–6ft); **S**: 2m (6ft)
❄❄❄ ◌ ◐ ☼

Sambucus nigra *'Eva'*

An ornamental elder tree grown for its attractive, finely cut, purple leaves, which turn vibrant red in autumn. The stunning, pink-tinged flowerheads in spring transform themselves into deep purple fruits later in the year. Also sold as 'Black Lace'.

H: 6m (20ft); **S**: 6m (20ft)
❄❄❄ ◌ ◐ ☼ ◑

Sorbus sargentiana

A broad, upright, slow-growing tree that is valued for its lovely orange and red autumn colours. These come from the large divided leaves and red berries. White flowers appear in early summer in broad clusters. Attractive to wildlife.

H: 6m (20ft); **S**: 10m (30ft)
❄❄❄ ◌ ◐ ☼ ◑ ♈

Sorbus vilmorinii

A spreading, shrubby tree grown for its dark red berries that fade as they age to pinkish-white. Clusters of white flowers appear in late spring to early summer. Prefers neutral to acid soil. The mountain ash (S. aucuparia) is also popular; both attract wildlife.

H: 5m (15ft); **S**: 5m (15ft)
❄❄❄ ◌ ◐ ☼ ◑ ♈

Stewartia sinensis

This small, deciduous tree has pale, flaking bark and leaves that turn an impressive deep red in autumn. The simple white flowers have a delicate fragrance. It prefers acidic soil. S. pseudocamellia is more popular, although slightly larger.

H: 6m (20ft); **S**: 3m (10ft)
❄❄❄ ◐ ☼ ◑ ♈

Styrax obassia
The fragrant snowbell is named for its flowers, which hang impressively on this round-headed tree in late spring. The large leaves turn yellow in autumn, and the peeling bark on the young wood is revealed in winter. Prefers acidic soil and a sheltered site.

H: 12m (40ft); **S**: 7m (22ft)
❄❄❄ ◊ ◗ ☼ ☼ ♉

Syringa vulgaris
'Madame Lemoine'
Forming small trees or large shrubs, lilacs offer an elegant display of fragrant flowers in later spring. This variety is an old favourite with spikes of creamy-yellow buds, unfurling into large, pure white double blooms.

H: 7m (22ft); **S**: 7m (22ft)
❄❄❄ ◊ ◗ ☼ ♉

Taxus baccata *'Fastigiata'*
Yew trees are among one of our most revered and ancient evergreen trees. The Irish yew has a narrow, upright habit, eventually forming a very distinguished, columnar shape, and produces small, red berries in summer. It is highly poisonous.

H: to 10m (30ft); **S**: 2m (6ft)
❄❄❄ ◊ ◗ ☼ ☼ ♉

Thuja occidentalis *'Rheingold'*
This is a bushy, dwarf conifer with attractively coloured foliage. Most of the year the leaves are golden yellow, but the juvenile growth is tinted pink, and in winter it takes on a bronze hue. The foliage has a fruity aroma. A good companion for heathers.

H: 1–2m (3–6ft); **S**: 3m (10ft)
❄❄❄ ◊ ◗ ☼ ♉

Trachycarpus fortunei
Adding a touch of the exotic to any garden design, this is one of the few palms suitable for a cool climate. Its large, fan-shaped leaves reach up to 1m (3ft) across and are held aloft on the attractive, fibrous, single trunk. Choose a sheltered site.

H: 10m (30ft); **S**: 2m (6ft)
❄❄❄ ◊ ☼ ♉

Tsuga canadensis *'Jeddeloh'*
There are many varieties of Eastern hemlock, and this is one of the most popular. A dwarf conifer with a squat habit, 'Jeddeloh' has attractive lime-green needles and interesting greyish-purple bark. Useful for evergreen interest in partially shaded areas.

H: 1.5m (5ft); **S**: 2m (6ft)
❄❄❄ ◊ ◗ ☼ ☼ ♉

Large shrubs

Abutilon vitifolium
'Veronica Tennant'
A semi-evergreen shrub that produces lots of bell-shaped, mauve flowers throughout summer. The lobed leaves are softly hairy. It can be slightly tender and benefits from being grown in a warm, sheltered position.

H: 5m (15ft); **S**: 2.5m (8ft)
❄❄ ◊ ☼ ♈

Amelanchier lamarckii
A stunning shrub with white, star-shaped blooms that cover the bare branches in early spring, followed by black berries. The young foliage in spring is coppery-red and matures to deep green in summer before turning scarlet red in autumn.

H: 10m (30ft); **S**: 12m (40ft)
❄❄❄ ◊ ◗ ☼ ☼ ♈

Buddleja alternifolia
With an arching, almost weeping habit, the long, slender branches of this shrub carry clusters of scented, purple-lilac flowers in summer. Regular pruning after flowering is advised to prevent branches from becoming tangled.

H: 4m (12ft); **S**: 4m (12ft)
❄❄❄ ◊ ◗ ☼ ☼ ♈

Buddleja davidii *'Royal Red'*
These buddlejas are fast-growing, tough, late-summer flowering shrubs, suitable for difficult sites, particularly chalk. They are superb for attracting beneficial insects, and respond well to hard pruning in early spring. 'Royal Red' has dark red-purple flowers.

H: 3m (10ft); **S**: 5m (15ft)
❄❄❄ ◊ ◗ ☼ ☼ ♈

Buddleja globosa
This buddleja is a vigorous, upright shrub forming small, orange-yellow balls of fragrant flowers in early summer. It has semi-evergreen foliage and is suitable for chalky soil. It prefers a sunny position and does not respond well to hard pruning.

H: 5m (15ft); **S**: 5m (15ft)
❄❄❄ ◊ ☼ ☼ ♈

Camellia *'Cornish Snow'*
Camellias are big, evergreen, spring-flowering shrubs for acid soils in sheltered sites. 'Cornish Snow' is studded with large numbers of small, cup-shaped white flowers, and has glossy, dark green leaves that are slightly bronze when young.

H: 3m (10ft); **S**: 1.5m (5ft)
❄❄❄ ◊ ◗ ☼ ♈

Ceanothus 'Cascade'
A vigorous, evergreen shrub with arching branches and glossy, dark green leaves. It bears masses of powder blue flowers from spring to early summer. It is slightly tender and benefits from a warm, sheltered position, such as against a sunny wall.

H: 4m (12ft); **S**: 4m (12ft)
❄❄ ◊ ◖ ☀

Chimonanthus praecox
This deciduous shrub forms pale creamy-yellow flowers on its bare stems throughout winter, perfuming the air with intoxicating scent. It is suitable for training on a sunny wall. The fragrant winter stems can be cut for indoor displays.

H: 4m (12ft); **S**: 3m (10ft)
❄❄❄ ◊ ☀

Clerodendrum trichotomum
var. **fargesii**
Clusters of small white or pink buds open in early summer on this deciduous shrub to reveal fragrant white flowers. These then develop into tiny, turquoise berries, which are more profuse in this variety.

H: to 6m (20ft); **S**: to 6m (20ft)
❄❄❄ ◊ ☀ ♈

Cotinus coggygria 'Royal Purple'
Grown for its purple foliage, this shrub is known as the smoke bush because of its fluffy plumes of pale pink flowers borne above the foliage in summer, which create a smoke-like haze. The leaves turn orange and red in autumn before falling.

H: 5m (15ft); **S**: 5m (15ft)
❄❄❄ ◊ ◖ ☀ ☀ ♈

Elaeagnus pungens 'Maculata'
Often seen growing near the coast because of its ability to withstand the salty winds, this is an attractive, evergreen foliage shrub. The leaves are splashed with gold down the centre. The insignificant but fragrant flowers appear in autumn.

H: 4m (12ft); **S**: 5m (15ft)
❄❄❄ ◊ ☀

Erica arborea var. alpina
Tree heathers make large evergreen shrubs with an upright habit. This variety produces an abundance of fragrant white flowers in spring. Like most heathers, it thrives in light sandy or loamy soil. Tree heathers respond well to hard pruning in spring.

H: 2m (6ft); **S**: 85cm (34in)
❄❄❄ ◊ ☀ ♈

Large shrubs

Garrya elliptica *'James Roof'*
This is an eye-catching evergreen shrub know as the silk-tassel bush for the extremely long catkins that hang from it during winter. The leathery leaves are greyish-green. It is slightly tender and therefore benefits from being grown against a sunny wall.

H: 4m (12ft); **S**: 4m (12ft)
❄❄❄ ○ ☼ ◐ 🏆

Hamamelis *x* intermedia *'Pallida'*
Considered to be the finest of all witch hazels, 'Pallida' produces fragrant, sulphur yellow blooms along its bare branches in winter. The leaves turn pale yellow in autumn before falling. Although a large shrub, its size can be restricted by pruning.

H: 4m (12ft); **S**: 4m (12ft)
❄❄❄ ○ ◑ ☼ ◐ 🏆

Hippophae rhamnoides
Sea buckthorn is a spiny, deciduous shrub that thrives naturally in coastal regions. It forms clusters of bright orange berries and its sharp thorns make it an excellent boundary hedge. Only female plants produce berries, but plant both sexes for best results.

H: 6m (20ft); **S**: 6m (20ft)
❄❄❄ ○ ◑ ☼ 🏆

Hydrangea paniculata *'Praecox'*
These hydrangeas are upright, deciduous shrubs with large, creamy, cone-shaped flower clusters in late summer. The largest clusters are produced by pruning the stems back hard in early spring. 'Praecox' flowers from midsummer.

H: 3–7m (10–22ft); **S**: 2.5m (8ft)
❄❄❄ ○ ◑ ☼ ◐

Ilex aquifolium *'Silver Queen'*
Grown for its delightful green thorny foliage with a pale edge, this holly adds a splash of evergreen colour to the winter garden. Despite its name, this is a male holly without berries; only female plants produce berries. It makes a useful barrier or screen.

H: 10m (30ft); **S**: 4m (12ft)
❄❄❄ ○ ☼ ◐ 🏆

Jasminum nudiflorum
The rich yellow flowers on this deciduous shrub are a welcome sight in midwinter, before the leaves emerge. Due to a lax and arching habit it is ideal for training on a low wall or trellis, but it is not self-clinging so will need tying in.

H: 3m (10ft); **S**: 3m (10ft)
❄❄❄ ○ ◑ ☼ ◐ 🏆

Lonicera periclymenum 'Graham Thomas'

A deciduous, twining honeysuckle that perfumes the air throughout summer with its white tubular flowers that mature to yellow. It requires a structure such as a trellis or pergola to scramble over.

H: 7m (22ft); **S**: 7m (22ft)
❄❄❄ ◌ ◍ ☼ ◐ ♔

Mahonia x media 'Charity'

This fast-growing evergreen shrub has an upright habit and holly-like, spiny foliage. It produces sweetly scented, bright yellow flower spikes from late autumn through to early spring. Its size can be restricted by hard pruning after flowering.

H: to 5m (15ft); **S**: to 4m (12ft)
❄❄❄ ◌ ◍ ☼ ◐

Olearia macrodonta

The daisy bush is an attractive foliage plant with pale green, holly-like leaves. White flowers with yellow centres cover the plant in early summer. It is often grown as a hedge and suits coastal regions. A warm, sheltered wall helps in cold areas.

H: 6m (20ft); **S**: 5m (15ft)
❄❄❄ ◌ ◍ ☼ ♔

Osmanthus x burkwoodii

A dense evergreen shrub grown for its dark leaves and very fragrant clusters of tiny, creamy-white flowers, which appear from mid- to late spring. It is typically used to make an attractive hedge or screen. Trim in summer after flowering.

H: 3m (10ft); **S**: 3m (10ft)
❄❄❄ ◌ ◍ ☼ ◐ ♔

Philadelphus 'Virginal'

One of the tallest and most vigorous mock oranges, this deciduous shrub is grown for its fragrant, many-petalled, white, early summer flowers. Remove one-third of the old growth annually after flowering. Suitable for chalky soils.

H: 3m (10ft); **S**: 2.5m (8ft)
❄❄❄ ◌ ◍ ☼ ◐

Photinia x fraseri 'Red Robin'

An evergreen shrub that produces striking, deep red young foliage in spring on the branch tips. The mature foliage is glossy and dark green. It is suitable for growing as a specimen shrub or as a hedge. Inconspicuous flowers appear in spring.

H: 5m (15ft); **S**: 5m (15ft)
❄❄❄ ◌ ◍ ☼ ◐ ♔

Large shrubs

Phyllostachys nigra
Black bamboo forms a large, shrubby plant that is important architecturally as it offers a permanent structure in the garden. It has tall black, arching stems that look fantastic rustling in the wind. Ideal as a specimen or as a semi-transparent screen.

H: 3–5m (10–15ft); **S**: 2–3m (6–10ft)
❋❋❋ ◊ ◐ ☼ ☀ ♈ ♔

Pieris *'Forest Flame'*
An evergreen shrub that is grown for its attractive juvenile foliage in spring. The leaves are scarlet when young, changing to pink and finally green. Clusters of white, bell-shaped flowers in spring are another attractive feature. It requires slightly acidic soil.

H: 4m (12ft); **S**: 2m (6ft)
❋❋❋ ◊ ◐ ☼ ☀ ♔

Prunus lusitanica
The Portuguese laurel can become a very large shrub with dark, evergreen foliage. Each leaf has a reddish stalk. The white, scented flowers develop into red fruits that mature to purple. It makes an attractive hedge and is suitable for chalky soils.

H: to 10m (30ft); **S**: to 10m (30ft)
❋❋❋ ◊ ◐ ☼ ☀ ♔ ♈

Pyracantha *'Orange Glow'*
Clusters of sumptuous, bright orange autumn berries and white spring flowers are the reasons for growing this evergreen shrub. It has a vigorous, dense and spiny habit, and can be grown against a wall or fence, or planted as a barrier hedge.

H: 3m (10ft); **S**: 3m (10ft)
❋❋❋ ◊ ◐ ☼ ☀ ♔

Rhododendron rex *subsp.* fictolacteum
One of the most striking large-leaved rhododendrons, in spring it bears impressive creamy-white trusses with crimson blotches in the centre. The new growth in summer is covered with a bronze dusting. It requires acid soil.

H: to 3m (10ft); **S**: to 3m (10ft)
❋❋❋ ◐ ◊ ☀ ♔

Rhus typhina
Autumn is the time for this shrub or small tree, owing to the spectacular foliage display of fiery reds and oranges. Female plants produce strange-looking, velvety, crimson fruits, hence the name velvety sumach, or stag's horn sumach.

H: 5m (15ft); **S**: 6m (20ft)
❋❋❋ ◊ ◐ ☼ ☀ ♔

Rosa *'Albertine'*
Deservedly still one of the most popular ramblers, this old favourite produces beautiful coppery-pink roses with a lovely fragrance. It flowers in midsummer and has a thorny, arching habit. Allow it to ramble up and over walls, fences and even flowerbeds.

H: 5m (15ft); **S**: 4m (12ft)
❁❁❁ ◊ ◑ ☼ ♈ ♉

Rosa *'New Dawn'*
This vigorous climbing rose produces fragrant, pale pink double flowers from midsummer and is ideal for covering walls or fences. Train the young stems horizontally to stimulate more flowers. It tolerates partial shade and a wide range of soils.

H: 5m (15ft); **S**: 5m (15ft)
❁❁❁ ◊ ◑ ☼ ◐ ♈ ♉

Tamarix ramosissima *'Pink Cascade'*
Producing large, arching plumes, this deciduous shrub is hardier than it looks, and is suitable for windy and coastal sites. Huge, feathery rich pink flowers appear in late summer. Prune in early spring to restrict its size.

H: 5m (15ft); **S**: 5m (15ft)
❁❁❁ ◊ ◑ ☼

Viburnum *x* **bodnantense** *'Dawn'*
Eventually making a large, upright shrub, this viburnum is grown for its sweetly scented, light pink flowers which form on bare stems during winter. The size can be restricted by removing a quarter of the older wood at the base after flowering.

H: 3m (10ft); **S**: 2m (6ft)
❁❁❁ ◊ ◑ ☼ ◐ ♉

Viburnum opulus
Commonly seen in hedgerows, the guelder rose is a vigorous, deciduous shrub with large white flowers in late spring, followed by abundant bunches of translucent red berries in autumn. The leaves turn red in autumn. Ideal for a wildlife hedge.

H: 5m (15ft); **S**: 4m (12ft)
❁❁❁ ◊ ◑ ☼ ◐

Viburnum tinus *'Eve Price'*
This popular evergreen shrub earns its keep in the garden by providing an all-year show. Pretty pink buds in late summer are succeeded by pinkish elder-like flowers from late autumn until spring. Dark blue berries follow. It has a dense, bushy habit.

H: 3m (10ft); **S**: 3m (10ft)
❁❁❁ ◊ ◑ ☼ ◐ ♉

Medium-sized shrubs

Abelia x grandiflora

A graceful flowering shrub with an attractive arching habit that retains its glossy dark green leaves throughout winter, except in very cold areas. The pale pink, scented flowers appear in early summer and last until autumn. Capable of becoming a large shrub.

H: to 3m (10ft); **S**: to 4m (12ft)
❄❄❄ ◊ ☼ ♈

Berberis thunbergii *'Rose Glow'*

This deciduous barberry has eye-catching purple leaves with a pinkish mottled effect on the surface. It forms small yellow flowers in spring, followed by red berries. Due to its dense and thorny habit, it is useful as a colourful, informal hedge or barrier.

H: 1m (3ft) or more; **S**: 2.5m (8ft)
❄❄❄ ◊◑ ☼ ◐ ♈

Brachyglottis *'Sunshine'*

This plant is primarily grown for its silvery-grey foliage and stems, although it also bears yellow daisy-like summer flowers. This is a sun-worshipping plant that can be clipped to form a low-growing hedge. It is tolerant of coastal conditions.

H: 1.5m (5ft); **S**: 2m (6ft)
❄❄❄ ◊ ☼ ♈

Callicarpa bodinieri *'Profusion'*

This deciduous shrub is highly valued for its stunning bright violet berries which appear in autumn. They are often used in floral displays. It also has eye-catching bronze young foliage in spring and clusters of pinky-purple flowers through summer.

H: to 3m (10ft); **S**: 2.5m (8ft)
❄❄❄ ◊ ☼ ♈

Callistemon citrinus

The crimson bottlebrush is an evergreen, sun-loving shrub, named for its bristly red flower spikes that form at the end of long, slender branches. The foliage is narrow and long with a subtle lemon fragrance when crushed.

H: 1.5m (5ft) or more; **S**: 1.5m (5ft)
❄❄ ◊ ☼

Chamaerops humilis

The dwarf fan palm is one of the few hardy palm trees. With a bushy, slow-growing habit, and evergreen, fan-like leaves, it makes a great focal point for a small garden. It needs a sheltered position, or grow in a pot and move to a cool place indoors over winter.

H: 2–3m (6–10ft); **S**: 1–2m (3–6ft)
❄❄ ◊ ☼ ♈

Choisya ternata *Sundance*
A colourful evergreen shrub with
bright yellow foliage that can lighten
the corner of any garden. The leaves
are slightly darker when grown in the
shade. Requires a sheltered position
in very cold areas, such as against a
sunny wall.

H: 2.5m (8ft); **S**: 2.5m (8ft)
❄❄ ◌ ◑ ☼ ◑ ♀

Cornus sanguinea
'Winter Beauty'
This dogwood is grown for winter
display. Its bright orange stems with
red tips reveal themselves once the
leaves have fallen. Prune hard in
spring for the best results. It will
make a big shrub if not pruned.

H: to 3m (10ft); **S**: to 2.5m (8ft)
❄❄❄ ◑ ◌ ☼

Corylopsis pauciflora
A graceful, deciduous shrub ideal for
a lightly shaded area of the garden.
It produces pale yellow, fragrant
flowers on its bare stems in early
to mid-spring. Keep pruning to a
minimum as this can often ruin its
attractive natural shape.

H: 1.5m (5ft); **S**: 2.5m (8ft)
❄❄❄ ◌ ◑ ◑ ♀

Daphne bholua
'Jacqueline Postill'
Daphnes are grown for their heady,
late winter fragrance. This one is
evergreen and slow-growing, making
it ideal for a small garden. The
scented winter flowers are white
and pink. Do not prune hard.

H: 3m (10ft); **S**: 1.5m (5ft)
❄❄❄ ◌ ◑ ◑ ♀

Desfontainea spinosa
This choice evergreen flowering shrub
deserves pride of place in any garden
with acidic soil. It has holly-like,
glossy dark green foliage, and in mid-
to late summer produces impressive
tubular yellow and red flowers. It
prefers slight shade.

H: 2m (6ft); **S**: 2m (6ft)
❄❄ ◌ ◑ ◑ ♀

Deutzia x hybrida *'Mont Rose'*
Studded with small pale pink flowers
in early summer, this deciduous shrub
is easy to grow. It forms a compact,
upright shape and is ideal for a shrub
border or mixed with perennial
plants. After flowering, prune out
one-third of the older wood.

H: 1.2m (4ft); **S**: 1.2m (4ft)
❄❄❄ ◌ ◑ ☼ ◑ ♀

Medium-sized shrubs

Enkianthus cernuus f. rubens

Preferring acidic soil, also loved by rhododendrons and camellias, this is a medium to large, deciduous shrub that produces a colourful display of deep red, bell-shaped flowers in late spring. The leaves turn red and purple in autumn.

H: 2.5m (8ft); **S**: 2.5m (8ft)
✻✻✻ ◐ ☀ ☼ ♔

Escallonia 'Apple Blossom'

This compact, evergreen shrub is perfect as a free-standing feature in a small garden due to its slow-growing habit. It is also a popular choice for a hedge or windbreak. It produces pinkish-white flowers in summer. Suitable for coastal conditions.

H: 2.5m (8ft); **S**: 2.5m (8ft)
✻✻✻ ○ ☀ ♔

Euonymus alatus

A deciduous shrub valued mainly for its autumn display, when the green foliage turns a spectacular crimson and scarlet, and purple and red fruits split open to reveal orange seed. A great plant for the back of a mixed border or small woodland garden.

H: 2m (6ft); **S**: 3m (10ft)
✻✻✻ ○◐ ☀ ☼ ♔

Exochorda x macrantha 'The Bride'

This deciduous shrub produces a profusion of white flowers on its long arching stems in late spring. Due to its short flowering period, it's best grown amongst other flowering shrubs in a mixed border. Remove some of the older wood each spring.

H: 2m (6ft); **S**: 3m (10ft)
✻✻✻ ○ ☀ ☼ ♔

Fatsia japonica

Japanese aralia is an evergreen architectural shrub with luxuriant, large, glossy leaves. It gives an exotic theme and is happy in either sun or shade. Spherical white flowerheads form in autumn. Ideal for a small city garden as it tolerates pollution.

H: to 3m (10ft); **S**: to 3m (10ft)
✻✻✻ ○◐ ☀ ☼ ♔

Forsythia x intermedia 'Lynwood Variety'

A deciduous, upright shrub that bears a mass of vivid yellow flowers in early spring before the leaves appear. It makes a great informal hedge. Remove one-third of the older growth after flowering to restrict its size.

H: to 3m (10ft); **S**: to 3m (10ft)
✻✻✻ ○◐ ☀ ☼ ♔

Fuchsia magellanica
This popular shrub produces a mass of long, elegant purple and red flowers through summer. It is hardier than most other fuchsias, but after an extremely cold winter, it should be cut back to ground level. It is often grown as a flowering hedge.

H: to 3m (10ft); **S**: 2–3m (6–10ft)
❄❄ ◊ ◐ ☼ ☼

Gaultheria mucronata *'Wintertime'*
Impressive, waxy white berries in autumn and winter are the reason for growing this evergreen, spreading shrub. It produces small white flowers in late spring and prefers neutral to acid soil. A male plant nearby ensures a good crop of berries.

H: 1.2m (4ft); **S**: 1.2m (4ft)
❄❄❄ ◊ ◐ ☼ ☼ ♆

Hibiscus syriacus *'Diana'*
Hardy hibiscus are ideal for providing large, blowsy blooms late in the season when most other flowers have disappeared. Those of 'Diana' are extra large and pure white. The size of this plant can be restricted by hard pruning in early spring.

H: to 3m (10ft); **S**: 2m (6ft)
❄❄❄ ◊ ◐ ☼ ♆

Hydrangea arborescens *'Annabelle'*
Huge, white flowerheads from midsummer into autumn make this upright, deciduous shrub a valuable asset in any garden. Restrict the size by cutting to a low framework annually in early spring.

H: 2.5m (8ft); **S**: 2.5m (8ft)
❄❄❄ ◊ ◐ ☼ ☼ ♆

Hydrangea macrophylla *'Mariesii Perfecta'*
Also sold as 'Blue Wave', this is a rounded, deciduous shrub grown for its blue, showy, lacecap flowers from mid- to late summer. Leave the flowerheads on over winter to protect the plant from frost damage.

H: 2m (6ft); **S**: 2.5m (8ft)
❄❄❄ ◊ ◐ ☼ ☼ ♆

Hydrangea quercifolia
The oak-leaved hydrangea is named for the shape of its large and attractive leaves, which turn to bronze-purple in autumn before they fall. Large white, conical flowerheads, which fade to pink as they age, are produced during midsummer.

H: 2m (6ft); **S**: 2.5m (8ft)
❄❄❄ ◊ ◐ ☼ ☼ ♆

Medium-sized shrubs

Hypericum *'Hidcote'*

This evergreen flowering shrub produces large, cupped, bright yellow flowers for a long period throughout summer. It is a suitable plant for both sunny and shady spots and can be hard pruned in early spring to retain its shrubby, compact habit.

H: 1.2m (4ft); **S**: 1.5m (5ft)
❋❋❋ ◊ ◐ ☼ ◑ ♧

Kalmia latifolia

The calico bush is an evergreen shrub for moist, acid soil and combines well with rhododendrons and camellias. It produces big clusters of pink flowers in late spring. Mulching the base with pine needles helps to retain moisture and acidity levels in the soil.

H: to 3m (10ft); **S**: to 3m (10ft)
❋❋❋ ◊ ☼ ◑ ♧

Kerria japonica *'Pleniflora'*

A deciduous, spring-flowering shrub that grows well in most gardens.It produces large, double, pompon-like yellow flowers on tall, arching stems. Restrict its spreading, suckering habit by regularly digging around the plant to sever stray roots.

H: 3m (10ft); **S**: 3m (10ft)
❋❋❋ ◊ ◐ ☼ ◑ ♧

Kolkwitzia amabilis *'Pink Cloud'*

The beauty bush produces bell-shaped, pale pink flowers in late spring on long, arching branches. It is any easy plant to grow but can be invasive due to its suckering habit. Prune after flowering by removing about one-third of the old wood.

H: to 3m (10ft); **S**: 4m (12ft)
❋❋❋ ◊ ☼ ♧

Lavatera x clementii *'Barnsley'*

Tree mallows are reliable garden shrubs, providing a plentiful display of pink or white flowers through summer. 'Barnsley' has white flowers that age to pale pink. Mallows establish quickly and are suitable for most sites, including coastal gardens.

H: 2m (6ft); **S**: 2m (6ft)
❋❋❋ ◊ ◐ ☼

Lonicera fragrantissima

This is a useful border shrub with tubular, creamy-white scented flowers from winter until early spring. It is semi-evergreen and will tolerate some shade, but prefers sun. Bring sprays of the cut flowers inside during winter to scent rooms.

H: 2m (6ft); **S**: 3m (10ft)
❋❋❋ ◊ ◐ ☼ ◑

Lonicera nitida *'Baggesen's Gold'*
Whilst most honeysuckles are grown for the scented flowers, this shrubby, evergreen one is valued for its bright yellow foliage made up of tiny leaves. A great plant for hedging or topiary, it is ideal for a city garden due to its tolerance of pollution.

H: 1.5m (5ft); **S**: 1.5m (5ft)
❄❄❄ ◊ ◑ ☼ ◑ ♈

Lupinus arboreus
The tree lupin is a spectacular, sun-loving shrub that produces spikes of pale yellow, fragrant flowers in early summer. It grows quickly and has a sprawling habit, which can be kept in check by cutting back after flowering. It will suit coastal conditions.

H: 2m (6ft); **S**: 2m (6ft)
❄❄ ◊ ☼ ♈

Myrtus communis *'Flore Pleno'*
The common myrtle is a sun-loving, evergreen shrub with aromatic foliage. It produces a profusion of fragrant white flowers in late summer; on this variety they are like small pompons. It benefits from a sheltered position in cooler climates.

H: to 3m (10ft); **S**: to 3m (10ft)
❄❄ ◊ ☼

Nandina domestica
The so-called heavenly bamboo bears little resemblance to a bamboo. It forms a medium-sized, evergreen clump with white flowers in spring, followed by red berries. The foliage has attractive red tints in autumn. It requires minimal pruning.

H: 2m (6ft); **S**: 1.5m (5ft)
❄❄ ◊ ◑ ☼ ♈

Pleioblastus viridistriatus
This evergreen bamboo offers permanent structure in the garden with its stunning gold and green foliage, and purple-green canes. It looks superb among shrubs or grasses, but as it can be invasive it may be best in a container.

H: 1.5m (5ft); **S**: 1.5m (5ft)
❄❄❄ ◊ ◑ ☼ ♈

Rhododendron *'Hydon Dawn'*
A compact evergreen shrub that produces frilly, pale pink flowers in spring. Its glossy dark green leaves are covered with a whitish powder (indumentum). An ideal plant for brightening a dappled corner of a garden, but it must have acid soil.

H: 1.5m (5ft); **S**: 1.5m (5ft)
❄❄❄ ◊ ☼ ◑ ♈

Medium-sized shrubs

Rhododendron
'Purple Splendour'
This medium to large, evergreen flowering shrub has showy, rich purple spring flowers with dark markings in the throats. It tolerates full sun but requires acid soil and can be prone to mildew.

H: to 3m (10ft); **S**: to 3m (10ft)
❄❄❄ ◐ ☼ ☀ ♔

Rhododendron *'Yellow Hammer'*
This upright, evergreen flowering shrub produces masses of small, pale yellow, tubular flowers in spring and then a later flush in autumn. It prefers light, dappled shade and requires acid soil, but unlike many rhododenrons, it tolerates full sun.

H: 2m (6ft); **S**: 2m (6ft)
❄❄❄ ◐ ☼ ☀ ♔

Ribes sanguinium
'Pulborough Scarlet'
Flowering currants are upright, deciduous shrubs grown for their attractive clusters of red flowers that appear in mid-spring. Remove some of the older stems after flowering to keep this variety in check.

H: to 3m (10ft); **S**: 2.5m (8ft)
❄❄❄ ◐ ◐ ☼ ♔

Rosa gallica *'Versicolor'*
This is an attractive rose producing a very distinctive, many-petalled flower streaked with dark and pale pink, with a yellow centre. Due to its fairly compact habit it can be used to create a striking informal hedge. It is named the Rosa mundi rose.

H: 1m (3ft); **S**: 1m (3ft)
❄❄❄ ◐ ◐ ☼ ♔

Rosmarinus officinalis
'Miss Jessopp's Upright'
Rosemary is grown for its aromatic evergreen foliage, which can be used in cooking. It produces blue flowers in spring. An essential plant for the herb garden that is often used for hedging. Trim after flowering.

H: 2m (6ft); **S**: 2m (6ft)
❄❄❄ ◐ ☼ ♔

Rubus cockburnianus *'Goldenvale'*
A deciduous, thicket-forming shrub grown for its winter display of ghostly white stems. An added benefit of this variety is its golden leaves which appear in spring and persist until autumn. In summer it produces purple flowers followed by purple fruits.

H: 2.5m (8ft); **S**: 2.5m (8ft)
❄❄❄ ◐ ◐ ☼ ☀ ♔

Sarcococca confusa

A superb choice for a shady location, this evergreen shrub is grown mainly for the small but very fragrant flowers that appear in winter. Black berries follow. Plant close to a doorway in a container, or clip it into a low hedge. It tolerates air pollution.

H: 2m (6ft); **S**: 1m (3ft)
❄❄❄ ◐ ☀ ◑ ♀

Skimmia japonica *'Rubella'*

A useful evergreen, dome-shaped shrub with attractive oval leaves. This is a male form, so produces no berries. Instead it bears extremely fragrant white flowers in spring. It is capable of becoming quite large if not clipped.

H: to 3m (10ft) or more; **S**: 3m (10ft)
❄❄❄ ◐ ☀ ◑ ♀

Spiraea *x* vanhouttei

A showy deciduous shrub for a mixed border, named bridal wreath for the masses of white, early summer flowers that show up nicely against the blue-green leaves. It has arching stems and is often used to create an informal hedge. Trim after flowering.

H: 2m (6ft); **S**: 1.5m (5ft)
❄❄❄ ◐ ☀

Viburnum davidii

A popular evergreen shrub with attractive dark green, deeply veined, leathery leaves. White flowers appear in spring, but it is only the female forms that produce the decorative metallic blue berries. Grow both sexes for a reliable show of fruits.

H: 1.5m (5ft); **S**: 1.5m (5ft)
❄❄❄ ◐ ◐ ☀ ♀

Weigela *'Florida Variegata'*

This is an easy-to-grow, deciduous shrub with tubular, dark pink flowers that appear in early summer. The green leaves are edged with cream, which give interest when the plant is not in flower. Remove one-third of the older growth after flowering.

H: 2.5m (8ft); **S**: 2.5m (8ft)
❄❄❄ ◐ ◐ ☀ ♀

Yucca gloriosa

Spanish dagger is a wonderful architectural plant ideal for growing in a courtyard garden or a dry, sunny border. It has bluish-green, sharply pointed leaves and produces very large panicles of white bell-like flowers in summer.

H: 2m (6ft); **S**: 2m (6ft)
❄❄❄ ◐ ☀ ♀

Small shrubs

Artemisia *'Powis Castle'*
This feathery, aromatic shrub has attractive, finely divided, silver foliage that forms a lovely billowing clump. The flowers are insignificant and often do not appear. It may not survive in cold areas. A good evergreen shrub for the herb garden.

H: 60cm (24in); **S**: 90cm (36in)
❄❄ ◊ ☼ ♈

Buxus sempervirens *'Suffruticosa'*
Often used as a small formal hedge, the box plant is a small-leaved, evergreen foliage shrub that can also be clipped into shapes. This form is very dense and slow growing, which makes it particularly good for fine topiary work.

H: to 1m (3ft); **S**: to 1.5m (5ft)
❄❄❄ ◊ ◐ ☼ ◑ ♈

Calluna vulgaris *'Kinlochruel'*
Heathers are distinctive, low-growing, evergreen flowering shrubs that are also valued for their foliage colours. This variety forms bright, double white summer flowers, and during winter the foliage becomes bronze. Trim in spring to keep neat.

H: 25cm (10in); **S**: 40cm (16in)
❄❄❄ ◊ ☼ ♈

Caryopteris x clandonensis
This lovely small shrub has beautiful blue flowers in late summer and early autumn above decorative, aromatic silvery-green foliage. 'Heavenly Blue' is popular for its intensely coloured flowers. Keep compact by cutting back to low buds in spring.

H: to 1m (3ft); **S**: to 1.5m (5ft)
❄❄❄ ◊ ☼

Chaenomeles x superba *'Crimson and Gold'*
Named for its red flowers with golden anthers, the dazzling blooms of this flowering quince first appear on the bare, spiny branches in spring. Grow as a free-standing shrub or train against a wall.

H: to 1m (3ft); **S**: to 1.5m (5ft)
❄❄❄ ◊ ☼ ◑ ♈

Cistus x lenis *'Grayswood Pink'*
A very hardy, drought-tolerant rock rose with a spreading habit. Its light pink flowers are borne in profusion during summer and are attractive to butterflies. A versatile shrub suitable for poor soils, as ground cover, in patio containers, or by sunny walls.

H: to 1m (3ft); **S**: to 1.5m (5ft)
❄❄❄ ◊ ☼ ♈

Cotoneaster horizontalis
This low-growing, deciduous shrub is excellent for covering walls and banks, and is also suitable as ground cover. Cotoneaster plants have wonderful red berries in the autumn, which follow the small white summer flowers; both attract wildlife.

H: to 1m (3ft); **S**: 1.5m (5ft) or more
❄❄❄ ◊ ◑ ☼ ◔ ♈

Erica carnea *'Springwood White'*
Winter heaths are pretty, winter-flowering, evergreen shrubs. 'Springwood White' bears masses of white flowers above the bright green foliage and is a vigorous grower. There are many other forms, some with pink flowers or golden foliage.

H: 25cm (10in); **S**: to 55cm (22in)
❄❄❄ ◊ ☼ ♈

Euonymus fortunei
'Emerald 'n' Gold'
This evergreen foliage shrub can be grown to cover a wall or fence, as ground cover, or as a free-standing shrub. This form has gold-variegated leaves; other forms with different coloured leaves are also popular.

H: 60cm (24in); **S**: 90cm (36in)
❄❄❄ ◊ ◑ ☼ ◔ ♈

Hebe *'Red Edge'*
A neat, gently spreading shrub grown for its red-edged, greyish leaves that are topped by short spikes of lilac-blue flowers in summer. Its evergreen foliage makes it useful in containers, particularly in winter when the leaves are more strongly tinged with red.

H: 45cm (18in); **S**: 60cm (24in)
❄❄ ◊ ☼ ◔ ♈

Juniperus communis *'Compressa'*
This juniper is a slow-growing evergreen conifer with blue-green, aromatic foliage. It is useful for providing winter structure in the garden and can be grown in a container. 'Hibernica' is similar, but slightly more vigorous.

H: to 80cm (32in); **S**: 45cm (18in)
❄❄❄ ◊ ◑ ☼ ◔ ♈

Lavandula angustifolia *'Hidcote'*
This lavender is a mass of blue-purple aromatic flowers during summer. It makes an excellent low-growing evergreen hedge for border edging. Shear off the flowerheads after flowering, then trim closely in spring to keep the growth compact.

H: 60cm (24in); **S**: 75cm (30in)
❄❄❄ ◊ ☼ ◔ ♈

Small shrubs

Lavandula stoechas

French lavender is a compact evergreen shrub with distinctive, dark purple flowerheads that are topped by a couple of rose-purple "wings" or "ears". The unusual flowers appear over a long period in summer above silvery foliage. Trim after flowering.

H: 60cm (24in); **S**: 60cm (24in)
❄❄❄ ◊ ☼ ♆

Phygelius x rectus *'African Queen'*

Cape fuchsia has tubular red flowers during summer, which hang down from the upward-curving branches. Treat it as a perennial and cut back almost to ground level in spring. 'Moonraker' has cream flowers; 'Devil's Tears' has red-pink flowers.

H: to 1m (3ft); **S**: 1.2m (4ft)
❄❄ ◊ ◊ ☼ ♆

Pittosporum tenuifolium *'Tom Thumb'*

Many forms of this evergreen shrub have variegated foliage and make an attractive focal point. 'Tom Thumb' is a very compact form, with bronze-purple leaves that emerge light green in spring, giving a two-tone effect.

H: to 1m (3ft); **S**: 60cm (24in)
❄❄ ◊ ◊ ☼ ☼ ♆

Potentilla fruticosa *'Primrose Beauty'*

Shrubby cinquefoils are attractive small shrubs with pretty, five-petalled flowers in summer. They are usually yellow, and this form matches the yellow of primroses; white-, red- and pink-flowered forms also exist.

H: to 1m (3ft); **S**: 1.5m (5ft)
❄❄❄ ◊ ☼ ♆

Rhododendron *'Vuyk's Rosyred'*

This dwarf, evergreen azalea has small leaves and bears a profusion of funnel-shaped, deep rosy-pink flowers in mid-spring. It is deservedly popular and would suit a patio container. Acid soil is essential, but it does tolerate full sun.

H: 75cm (30in); **S**: 1.2m (4ft)
❄❄❄ ◊ ☼ ☼ ♆

Rosa *Gertrude Jekyll*

A very popular hybrid tea rose with large, deep pink, cup-shaped flowers through summer. All hybrid tea roses respond well to hard pruning in early spring, resulting in better flowers and more compact growth; cut all stems back to 15cm (6in) above the soil.

H: to 1m (3ft) or more; **S**: 1m (3ft)
❄❄❄ ◊ ◊ ☼ ♆

Rosa *Iceberg*
A classic floribunda rose with double creamy or pure white flowers that appear freely right through summer. Floribunda roses respond to hard pruning in early spring; aim to leave a framework of 6 to 8 stems 20–30cm (8–12in) above the ground.

H: 80cm (32in); **S**: 65cm (26in)
❄❄❄ ◊ ◊ ☼ ♈

Rosa *'Just Joey'*
A floribunda rose with double, muskily fragrant, copper-pink flowers from summer to autumn. Floribunda roses respond to hard pruning in early spring; aim to leave a framework of 6 to 8 stems 20–30cm (8–12in) above the ground.

H: 75cm (30in); **S**: 70cm (28in)
❄❄❄ ◊ ◊ ☼ ♈

Rosa *Sexy Rexy*
An outstanding floribunda rose that flowers effortlessly right through summer. It has good, healthy foliage and lovely, showy pink flowers. Prune hard in early spring; aim to leave a framework of 6 to 8 stems 20–30cm (8–12in) above the ground.

H: 70cm (28in); **S**: 60cm (24in)
❄❄❄ ◊ ◊ ☼ ♈

Salvia officinalis *'Purpurascens'*
Purple sage is simply a colourful form of the common sage, and like that plant is ideal for a herb garden, where contrasting foliage is desired. The foliage is aromatic and can be used in cooking. Forms with other foliage colours are available.

H: to 80cm (32in); **S**: 1m (3ft)
❄❄ ◊ ◊ ☼ ☼ ♈

Santolina chamaecyparissus
Cotton lavender has aromatic, silvery-grey, evergreen foliage and bright yellow pompon flowers in summer. It can be grown as a low hedge or edging, and also in the mixed border. It is useful as a structural plant in the winter herb garden.

H: 50cm (20in); **S**: 1m (3ft)
❄❄ ◊ ☼ ♈

Thymus citriodorus *'Silver Queen'*
Lemon-scented thyme makes a low, rounded shrub with silvery foliage and masses of pale pink flowers throughout summer. Thyme is an essential plant in the herb garden as it is deliciously fragrant and a ready supply is useful for the kitchen.

H: to 30cm (12in); **S**: to 25cm (10in)
❄❄❄ ◊ ☼ ♈

Fruit trees and shrubs

Ficus carica *'Brown Turkey'*
'Brown Turkey' is the hardiest and most popular variety of fig in cool climates. It is ideally grown as a fan on a sunny wall, but in cold areas it should be cultivated in a pot and moved under cover in winter. Prune in spring or autumn.

H: 3m (10ft); **S**: 4m (12ft)
❄❄ ◊ ◐ ☼ ♆

Malus domestica *'Cox's Orange Pippin'*
Apple trees are ideal for small gardens as they can be grown on dwarfing rootstocks. 'Cox's Orange Pippin' is considered to be one of the tastiest apples with an attractive skin. It can be slightly prone to disease.

H: 10m (30ft); **S**: 6m (20ft)
❄❄❄ ◊ ◐ ☼

Prunus armeniaca *'Tomcot'*
Apricots require a warm, sheltered position to grow successfully. 'Tomcot' is one of the most reliable varieties for a cold climate. It has large, orangey-red fruit and an intense flavour. It should be pruned in spring or late summer.

H: 8m (25ft); **S**: 8m (25ft)
❄❄ ◊ ◐ ☼

Prunus cerasus *'Morello'*
'Morello' is a dark-skinned, self-fertile, acid cherry, suitable for cooking. It can be grown as a free-standing tree or as a fan on a north-facing wall. It should only be pruned from spring to late summer to avoid disease problems.

H: 8m (25ft); **S**: 8m (25ft)
❄❄❄ ◊ ◐ ☼ ◐ ♆

Prunus domestica *'Victoria'*
Plums are easy to grow, and where space is limited, they can be trained against a wall or a fence as a fan. 'Victoria' is reliable, self-fertile, and heavy cropping, and from mid-summer it produces pale red fruit with yellow flesh.

H: 8m (25ft); **S**: 8m (25ft)
❄❄❄ ◊ ◐ ☼ ♆

Prunus persica *'Rochester'*
'Rochester' is one of the most reliable peach varieties for a cool climate, but it needs the warmth of a south-facing wall. It has yellow flesh with a good flavour. All peaches are prone to peach leaf curl disease; shelter from rain and dew to prevent infection.

H: 8m (25ft); **S**: 8m (25ft)
❄❄ ◊ ◐ ☼ ♆

Pyrus communis *'Conference'*
Pears are soft-fleshed, juicy and delicious top fruits. Their early white blossom, however, can be susceptible to frost damage. In a small garden, they can be grown flat against a wall or fence. 'Conference' is a reliable, heavy cropper.

H: 15m (50ft); **S**: 10m (30ft)
❄❄❄ ◊ ◖ ☼ ♈

Ribes nigrum *'Ben Connan'*
Blackcurrants taste delicious when eaten fresh, cooked, or made into a cordial. 'Ben Connan' produces large blackcurrants, has resistance to mildew, and ripens early. Prune by removing one-third of the old growth at the base in winter.

H: 1m (3ft); **S**: 1m (3ft)
❄❄❄ ◊ ◖ ☼ ♈

Ribes rubrum *'Jonkheer van Tets'*
Redcurrants have a sharp flavour when eaten fresh, but they can be cooked in pies, made into fantastic jelly, or used to brighten up a dish. Grow them as an open-centred bush. This early variety is a heavy cropper with good flavour.

H: 1m (3ft); **S**: 1m (3ft)
❄❄❄ ◊ ◖ ☼ ☼ ♈

Ribes uva-crispa *'Invicta'*
One of the first fruits to crop in the year, gooseberries come in a range of colours, including red, white, green and yellow. 'Invicta' is a dual-purpose green fruit, which can be eaten fresh from the bush or used in cooking. It has vigour and disease resistance.

H: 1m (3ft); **S**: 1m (3ft)
❄❄❄ ◊ ◖ ☼ ☼ ♈

Rubus idaeus *'Glen Ample'*
This summer-fruiting raspberry has large, deep red, juicy berries. They are ideal for eating fresh from the plant, making into jam, or freezing. After fruiting the old canes should be cut down to ground level and the new canes tied in to a wire framework.

H: 1.5m (5ft); **S**: 2m (6ft)
❄❄❄ ◊ ◖ ☼ ☼ ♈

Vaccinium corymbosum *'Bluecrop'*
Blueberries are medium-sized shrubs that need acid soil. They grow best in groups to improve pollination. Mulch the base of the plant with pine needles each year to maintain acidity. 'Bluecrop' is an easy-to-grow, light blue variety with good flavour.

H: 1.5m (5ft); **S**: 1.5m (5ft)
❄❄❄ ◊ ◖ ☼

Index

Index

Acknowledgements

The publisher would like to thank the following for their kind permission to reproduce their photographs:

(Key: a-above; b-below/bottom; c-centre; f-far; l-left; r-right; t-top)

6-7: DK Images: Peter Anderson, Designer: Geoff Whiten/The Pavestone Garden/Chelsea Flower Show 2006. **11:** GAP Photos Ltd: Richard Bloom/Foggy Bottom Garden. **12:** Alamy Images: Holmes Garden Photos (t). **14-15:** Garden Picture Library: John Glover/Brook Farm Lodge Cottage, Surrey. **16:** DK Images: Peter Anderson, Designer: Tom Stuart-Smith/The Telegraph Garden/Chelsea Flower Show 2006. **17:** Garden Picture Library: Anne Hyde/Osler Road (b). **18:** DK Images: Peter Anderson, Designer:Chris Beardshaw/The Chris Beardshaw Garden/Chelsea Flower Show 2007 (bl). **20:** The Garden Collection: Nicola Stocken Tomkins (tr), DK Images: Peter Anderson, Designer: Roger Griffin (Amenity Trees & Landscapes)/Association of British Conifer Growers, Conifers by Design/Hampton Court Palace Flower Show 2007 (tl), Designers: Jeffery Hewitt & Edmund Colville/Living Values/Hampton Court Palace Flower Show 2007 (b). **21:** Marianne Majerus Photography: Designer: Declan Buckley (b). **22:** Garden Picture Library: Eric Crichton/Copeland Garden, NGS. **23:** DK Images: Steven Wooster, Designer: Tom Stuart-Smith/Laurent-Perrier, Harpers & Queen Garden/Chelsea Flower Show 2003 (b). **24:** The Garden Collection: Derek St Romaine, Designer: Polly Hamilton (t), DK Images: Brian North, Designer: Jamie Dunstan/Cater Allen Private Bank Garden/Tatton Park Flower Show 2007 (c), Steven Wooster, Designer: Christopher Bradley-Hole/Hortus Conclusus Garden/Chelsea Flower Show 2004 (b). **25 :** DK Images: Peter Anderson, Designer: Diarmuid Gavin & Stephen Reilly/The Westland Garden/Chelsea Flower Show 2007. **26:** DK Images: Peter Anderson, Designer: Andy Sturgeon/RHS Wisley Garden 2007 (t), Brian North, Designer: Lucy Hunter Garden Designs/A Private View/Tatton Park Flower Show 2007 (b). **27:** DK Images: Peter Anderson, Designer: Geoff Whiten/The Pavestone Garden/Chelsea Flower Show 2006 (t), Designer: Helen Williams/The Green & Light Garden/Hampton Court Palace Flower Show 2007 (b). **28:** The Garden Collection: Liz Eddison, Designer: Geoffrey Whiten, Chelsea Flower Show 2003 (bl), DK Images: Peter Anderson, Designer: Paul Stone Gardens/The 'I'll Drink to That' Garden/Hampton Court Palace Flower Show 2007 (tr), Designer: Chris Beardshaw/The Chris Beardshaw Garden/Chelsea Flower Show 2007 (br). **29:** DK Images: Steven Wooster, Chelsea Flower Show 2001. **60:** The Garden Collection: Liz Eddison. **67:** GAP Photos Ltd: Maddie Thornhill, West Dean Garden, West Sussex. **70:** crocus.co.uk (br). **71:** GAP Photos Ltd: John Glover. **72-3:** DK Images: Brian North, Designer: Sarah Eberle/600 Days with Bradstone/Chelsea Flower Show 2007 **74-5:** DK Images: Brian North, Designers: Harry Levy & Geoff Carter/Aughton Green Landscapes & The Big Pond Company, The Water Garden/Tatton Park Flower Show 2007. **77:** DK Images: Peter Anderson, Designers: R J Griffin, Amenity Trees & Landscapes/Association of British Conifer Growers, Cedrus and Friends/Hampton Court Palace Flower Show 2006. **79:** Garden Picture Library: Howard Rice. **83:** Garden Picture Library: Ron Evans. **108:** Garden Picture Library: Marie O'Hara, Bourton House, Glos. **116:** The Garden Collection: Derek St Romaine (bl). **134:** Caroline Reed (tr). **138:** Garden Picture Library: Mark Bolton (tr).

All other images © Dorling Kindersley. For further information see: www.dkimages.com

Dorling Kindersley would also like to thank the following:

Index: Jane Coulter

Hyde Hall and Rosemoor (www.rhs.org.uk) for photography locations.

Ashridge trees for supplying the bare root hedging plants (www.ashridgetrees.co.uk).

Topiary Arts for the topiary section (tel: 020 8894 2816;www.topiaryarts.com).